Teachers & Parents Together

Maureen Botrie / Pat Wenger

Pembroke Publishers Limited

© 1992 Pembroke Publishers Limited
538 Hood Road
Markham, Ontario
L3R 3K9

Canadian Cataloguing in Publication Data

Botrie, Maureen
  Teachers and parents together

Includes bibliographical references.
ISBN 0-921217-81-1

1. Parent-teacher relationships. 2. Education, Elementary – Parent participation. 3. Language and languages – Study and teaching (Elementary).
I. Wenger, Pat. II. Title.

LC230.B78 1992   371.1'03   C92-094758-1

Editor: Joanne Close
Design: John Zehethofer
Cover Photography: Ajay Photographics
Typesetting: Jay Tee Graphics Ltd.

This book was produced with the generous assistance of the Government of Ontario through the Ministry of Culture and Communications.

Printed and bound in Canada
9 8 7 6 5 4 3 2 1

Dedications

I dedicate this book to all the fine educators and parents who have influenced me and have permitted me to influence them. Also to that dynamic organization, my family — Jim, Jonathan, Olivia and Jenna whose love and support drive my work.

Maureen

To five caring men who have supported me with kindness and encouragement — my husband Ed, my two sons John and Adam, Merv Matier, Principal, Toronto Board of Education, and Ron Benson, Coordinator, Scarborough Language Centre.

Pat

Contents

Foreword

The sun was warm at midday as Maureen's daughters and her friends swam energetically between the beach and the raft. My two teenage sons were happily engaged elsewhere — one at camp, the other working as a lifeguard in Toronto. Maureen's son was earning money housepainting their home in the city.

Inside the cottage, Maureen and I were working at the pine table — lap top computer in place, and pens, paper, dictionaries, and reference texts strewn about. As the girls beckoned us to become the audience for their aqua show, we remarked on how much we were enjoying, at that moment, the best of all worlds. Here we were, as both parents and teachers, writing about what we know to be essential for all children's positive growth — the effective partnership of parents and educators. It is because we place inestimable value on these coeducational roles that we have written this book.

Our own classroom experiences, observations, and personal growth throughout our teaching years have clearly demonstrated that the teaching profession encounters many daily challenges. As a result, we need to dialogue often with colleagues and consider parents as collaborative partners if we and our students are to thrive.

CHAPTER ONE

Thoughts on Parental Involvement

"If you're not part of the solution, you're part of the problem"

Why Parental Involvement?

Greater positive parental involvement in education, through the school system and at home, may be the strongest single factor to promote student success.

Educators need to help parents recognize their importance in positively impacting children. A parent who consciously exhibits a positive attitude toward education shapes his/her child's attitudes towards school and potential future success. A child's attitude and perception of school drives his/her work habits, attention, and potential outcomes. If children see a home/school support system in place, it helps them to feel secure, directed, and confident.

Parents have a vested interest in seeing their children succeed. Therefore they are a committed resource requiring direction. Preventative models can be applied in both home and school when parents become stronger guides for their children. If we don't help parents understand how to support their child's learning, we affect equity of outcomes in education. Some of today's complex, fragmented, busy families need the school to offer guidance, direction, and support. The school is increasingly becoming the preventative/corrective nucleus for the community it serves.

Supportive, empowered parents make a teacher's work easier, not harder. When parents view the school's climate as "inviting", they become good public relations advocates for that school. Parents also offer educators important information about the local community and individual children. This information provides teachers with knowledge that influences teaching. Schools require parental support to provide active, enriched programs without the cost of additional educational support. As well, many school programs require parental investment and involvement in order to be successful, for example: home reading programs, homework policies, and values education. An adversarial parent group can create a negative force, effectively cancelling out the good work educators do with students.

Parents and educators need to recognize the fact that they *both* have a positive, supportive role to play. Warring home and school factions can have the same unfortunate impact on children as a parent custody battle. Parents and teachers acting negatively toward one another does not build a healthy climate for children and devalues education. Schools may want to clearly define what roles parents and educators play in order to lessen explosive reactions to issues from both parties. Everyone involved with students will be more rational, and coeducational support will be restored.

Beyond the Bake Sale by A. Henderson et al. (National Committee for Citizens in Education, 1986) promotes parental involvement and is written from the parents' perspective. It identifies hierarchically five levels of parental involvement:

1. Partners — parents who fulfill the requirements for children to be involved in school successfully, that is, send their children to school on time, offer bedtime routines, provide appropriate dress, nourish children adequately, respond to communications with the school, and so on.

2. Collaborators and Problem Solvers — parents who actively deal with home and school issues and work to solve an identified problem in collaboration with the school.

3. Audience — parents who appear at school to view a performance of one class or the whole school.

4. Supporters — parents who work in the school as parent volunteers.

5. Advisors and Codecision Makers — parents who help teachers to shape policies, hire staff, and so on.

The roles may not be as hierarchical as those listed above. Each role has a value depending on the needs of your school. If your school needs parents to become more informed about routines, attendance, basic parenting, and so on then "partners" is the area to focus on. If your school needs parents to become tutors and/or goal setters for children then focus on "collaborators". These kinds of parental involvement have direct impact on an individual student's school performance.

In schools where good public relations are essential, encourage parents to respond as an audience and as general school supporters. Schools that need extra hands in the classrooms and throughout the school to run their active programs would bring parents in as "supporters". If parents and teachers are interested in shaping policies, you may need to decide where to cooperatively direct your energies first. We suggest addressing areas that directly impact parents and teachers, for example, a homework policy.

It is also possible for different committees and individual teachers to be addressing these levels in various ways at the same time; schools are complex, dynamic organizations that perform different functions simultaneously. However, schools that have carefully considered the needs of the families should be able to determine an appropriate direction.

Dynamics to Consider

Parent education or group meetings offer greater numbers of parents the opportunity to understand current education. If parents are invited to the school early in the year so that programs can be explained as simply and concretely as possible, they will develop a more realistic view of the school and its goals. It is important to recognize that *all* parents have been part of an education system and therefore have their own views on education. Whenever possible, explain the curriculum to large groups of parents as this saves teacher energy and time. Education has undergone many changes during the past decade; parents need to understand the rationale for those changes before they will support them.

Before a new initiative is taken, consider how it will be perceived by the parents involved. Educators will benefit by stepping back and viewing change from the parents' perspective in order to diffuse potential possible conflict.

Parents also need to be honored by the school, especially those parents who directly contribute their time to its success. When you honor the parent, you honor the child. This is particularly important when dealing with inner-city families where cultures between home and school may be very different.

Schools must not be afraid to stand by their principles about learning when an issue with an aggressive parent arises. Some parents will use the school as a target if they are undergoing stressful experiences in their own lives or have had negative personal school experiences. School policies offer strength to educators and help to create clear messages. When all potential solutions have been assessed and a compromise on a critical issue can't be reached, parents could possibly consider changing schools. Educators who experience similar stress could also consider this option.

Parents may need to be involved in the educational process before, during, and after a program implementation. If a program will directly affect parents in any way, they should be involved in its shaping. When a program requiring parental support is in place, their feedback should be used to modify or continue its direction. Parental evaluation of meetings, new reporting procedures, and so on offer educators a view on what parents find most useful. We also need to have in place a process where parent groups can access staff meetings when issues overlap roles. Parents and teachers can problem solve around particular issues. If we "see" parents as having a legitimate voice, they will become more responsive to, and responsible for, education.

It is natural for parents to talk about the school and their child's education, even when we are not part of their conversation. We must accept this reality. If we make our schools inviting and promote a healthy interaction between teachers and parents, we have an opportunity to influence the tone of their talk.

Assessment/information about individual children needs to be given to parents in a specific, concrete, ongoing basis. The more information (e.g., writing folders) we collect throughout the year, the more we have to share with parents. If there are difficulties to be addressed, share information with parents early in the school year. Collaborative problem solving between home and school will help to create positive solutions — parental support can be the crucial catalyst.

Videotapes of classroom programming and special events offer parents who cannot visit classrooms insight into school curriculum. Parents will get a clear idea of a classroom and their child's perception by watching a video. Most families have a V.C.R. available; videos should be used by schools to deepen understanding.

Children also become more actively involved in learning when they realize their parents will be viewing their performance.

Some students see their parents as wielding negative power within a school. Children can then see themselves as powerful, omnipotent, negative forces. Teachers may be reluctant to deal with these students appropriately as they wish to avoid an aggressive parent. However, if these children are not dealt with at school fairly, their development becomes limited. This is not the outcome parents ultimately want.

Parents should be included in their child's celebration of learning. If we look for ways to invite parents to the school at the culmination of a learning experience, children have a supportive audience and parents have a real opportunity to view their child's learning. One of the most positive messages to children occurs when they see parents and teachers talking constructively together.

Programs offered within a school that help develop parents' knowledge can have a direct impact on the children they serve, especially inner-city parents, families new to the culture, or parents experiencing parenting problems. Parenting, computer, and literacy programs can support whole families.

When thinking about parents, we need to remember that all parents are individuals with their own views, experiences, and attitudes. We must respect this and not paint all parents with the same brush, especially if we have had negative experiences. Parents must also be reminded to see teachers as unique individuals with different teaching styles and strengths. The common threads between teachers and parents should be their interest, advocacy, and support for children.

Roles of Educators, Parents, and Children

We believe parents and educators play a crucial role in developing children. Together they provide a supportive safety net within which children can grow both at home and at school. Both groups are human and basically imperfect, so it is important that we work together to provide the most consistent support we can. Children also have responsibilities within the home and the school.

Role of Educators

* to look for the good in the parents;
* to consider how their actions would appear to parents, i.e., put themselves in their place and ask "How would a parent feel about this?";
* to think about how parents might be involved in the program and consider if they need to be consulted before a change takes place;
* to help parents understand current education, philosophy and practices;
* to remain supportive of the home in front of the child;
* to provide clear information to parents and children about school progress;
* to develop with parents ways they might help their child at home;
* to listen to the parents' point of view and understanding of the child;
* to accept the responsibility for working at school with each child, building on strengths and working on specific needs;
* to treat the parent(s) with respect *because they are the parent(s)*;
* to actively encourage parent participation in their children's learning and in the life of the school;
* to inform parents promptly and specifically about difficulties, both behaviorally and academically;
* to attempt to meet/talk with parents at times convenient for both;
* to be advocates for children;
* to provide good role models for children.

Role of Parents

* to look for the good in the teacher;
* to consider the teacher's perspective, to put themselves in the position of the teacher and think about how an action would be perceived by him/her, "If I was the teacher, how would I feel about this?";
* to remain supportive of the school in front of their children;
* to tell their children that school and education are important, as they will model parents' viewpoints;
* to approach the teacher *first* if difficulties arise;
* to treat the teacher with respect because *s/he is the teacher*;
* to listen to the teacher's point of view and understanding of the child;
* to inform educators of changing situations in the home which may have influenced learning;
* to accept the responsibility to help their child at home, supporting children's strengths and working on needs;
* to remember their child's needs cannot overwhelm the needs of a class;
* to meet/talk with teachers at convenient, appropriate times (e.g., not interrupting a lesson in class);
* to provide good role models for children.

Role of Children

* to become self-directed learners who take responsibility for their own learning;
* to seek help from both parents and teachers if required;
* to treat teachers and parents with respect because they are prime advocates and nurturers.

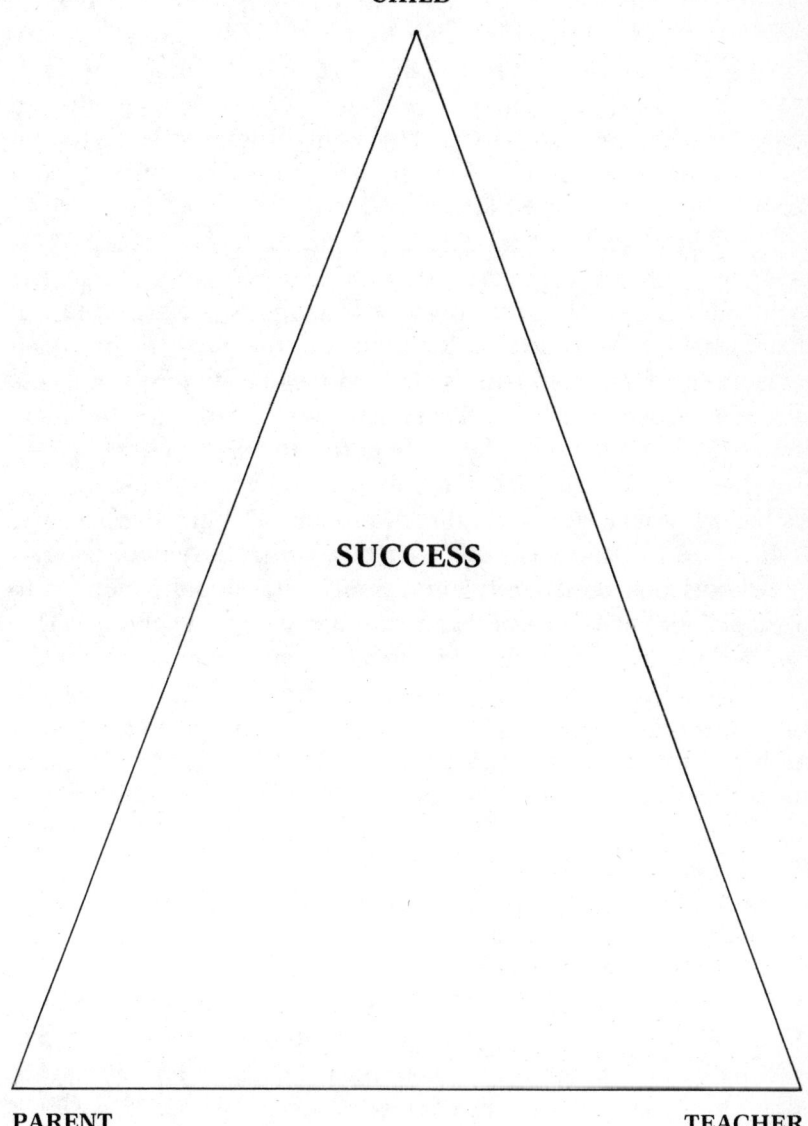

Guiding Principles

"Parental support for a school and its programs is often a matter of perception and attitude. A school that is not in the "top ten" may still be excellent if parents believe that it is."

M. Heller & M. Lundquist, Getting Parental Support
for Your School Principal

All teachers have beliefs about how students learn and what constitutes optimal learning environments. These beliefs drive the ways teachers physically arrange their classrooms, plan their programs, and interact with students. The varied, immediate decisions demanded in teaching require teachers to respond intuitively, based on their own principles of learning. However, the isolation of teaching situations can limit these beliefs about learning from being shared with others. Educators, without opportunities to articulate their beliefs and listen to the experiences of others in their schools, rely on their own motivation to develop professionally. The outcome may be educators with fragmented, polarized educational beliefs operating under the same roof, diminishing one another's effectiveness during the course of a student's progress through the school. Schools that structure opportunities for teachers to develop and grow provide benefits for all teachers. When teachers within a school collaboratively develop a common set of beliefs about learning, the direction of teaching practice becomes clearer and actions more consistent within the school itself.

Schools that collaboratively design policies and programs to reflect their beliefs send a much stronger message to parents. This unified message, articulated by teachers and written in policies, offers teachers support when talking with parents. Six teachers, in sequential years, who talk to parents about the social nature of learning create a strong statement. Four teachers who present to parents a workshop on the nature of writing within the school show uniformity. A written set of beliefs about learning that is shared with parents helps them view the school as a cohesive, holistic organization through which their child can move with some consistency. Remember, parents choose schools, not individual teachers.

Schools operate like any organization. The greater the communication between the personnel involved, the greater the chance of strengthening overall effectiveness. Principals who consciously organize these opportunities acknowledge both teachers' individual strengths and their need to grow together. Through the direction of a caring principal, a collaborative school can evolve that utilizes the talents of the personnel inside and outside of the school environment. S/he establishes a positive climate, models a high-energy level, programs for student success, encourages positive risk-taking, and invites all educational partners to flourish together.

Once these beliefs about learning are established, teachers can more confidently work with parents, knowing that the administration and other teaching staff support them. They can also use these beliefs independently as guideposts when planning for, interacting with, and evaluating students.

Wouldn't it be great if. . .

all principals modeled these behaviors.

Two Processes for Developing a Shared Vision

Consider this:

1. Each staff might work during a one- or two-day in-service to:

   - Collaboratively discuss the school's beliefs about learning. First, teachers write their individual beliefs before sharing them with a partner. Finally, the group shares them as a whole, and forms a common list of beliefs.
   - Identify what the school is doing to support these guiding principles of learning. This facilitates positive feelings about present programming, and helps other teachers become informed.
   - Identify the practices that promote the successful implementation of these principles of learning in the school.
   - Problem solve ways of affecting change.
   - Identify what the school is doing that *does not* support these beliefs. Discuss these practices to determine if they should be terminated.

or

2. Some staffs may find the following process more valuable:

   - During grade level meetings explore, articulate, and reflect together on classroom practices.

- Consider and discuss the two questions given below. What do you do to support listening, reading, writing, and so on in your grade six classroom? grade two classroom? How do your programs support the continuum of learning throughout the school?

From this pragmatic, practical approach teachers' beliefs will emerge. A small group forum creates a comfortable learning/sharing climate that promotes tolerance and acceptance of varying teaching philosophies.

If a parent/teacher handbook is a result of either process, invite a few parents to read the final draft. Parents can identify and clarify any teacher jargon that may confuse others. Including parents at this stage also offers them an opportunity to shape the final product. It says, "We value your involvement."

Reinforcing and Extending Your School's Beliefs

- Plan school directions to facilitate implementation and understanding of guiding principles and supporting practices, for example, parent and teacher workshops.
- Publicize these principles of the school for parents, teachers, and students.
- Include them on the parents' bulletin board, in a newsletter, or refer to them when welcoming new parents or addressing parent groups.
- Teachers can refer to a classroom set to guide their planning, teaching practice, and evaluation.
- Help students become aware of the principles so that they better understand the thinking behind teachers' decisions on programming, grouping, evaluation, and so on.
- Visitors, such as occasional staff and student teachers, assimilate more easily if they understand the school's focus and beliefs.

Each school's beliefs about learning may be different, reflecting the needs of the community, students, and particular strengths of individual schools. Uniqueness of schools, when articulated to parents, helps them decide if a school best suits the needs of their child and their family.

Informed parents who join a school community will be more supportive in the long run. The parent/school partnership becomes a win/win situation rather than a tug of war where each party tries to convince the other of the merit of their viewpoint(s).

The Parent Involvement Committee

The beliefs of a school can help determine its committee structure. Teachers can decide what areas to focus on to continue growth and establish appropriate committees. If a school believes that parental support is a crucial component for student success, a small parent involvement committee might think about ways to include parents in the school. The establishment of such a committee legitimizes this issue and helps raise teacher consciousness about relationships with parents. When committees report back to the whole group, other teachers begin to consider parent/teacher issues more consciously.

Each school will determine its own methods of strengthening ties with parents. The ways to involve parents will be as creative as the staff involved in the planning. Teachers will gradually take ownership as they are asked to consider the problem and generate creative solutions. The most effective ways of dealing with each parent group will become evident as ideas are created, implemented, and assessed.

If schools create Parent Involvement Committees they help shape their relationship with parents. Educators are less likely to present a knee-jerk reaction to a disgruntled parent, and will become aware of the parents' needs and the perspective of the school system. Schools, by establishing the committee, appear to place value on parents' voices. This perception helps to strengthen parent/school relationships.

Parent Involvement Committees might generate discussion around one or two of the following questions throughout the year. Parent inclusion recognizes that schools need their involvement to create policies to establish parental

- support,
- ownership,
- commitment,
- knowledge and understanding.

Parents and Teachers: Joint Partners in School Policy?

Consider the following questions. It might be helpful to jot down your thoughts. The resultant responses will give you an overview of parent/teacher relationships in your school.

- How do we address the needs of working parents? non-custodial parents? ESL parents?
- How do we involve parents in developing our initiatives and our school focus (e.g., school values policy)?
- How do we explain our evaluation criteria to parents?
- How can we help parents network with one another?
- How can we draw parents, in a meaningful way, into the school?
- How can parents help support the beliefs of the school?
- How are parents involved when the school is developing and/or implementing an initiative?
- How do we welcome new families to our school?
- How are parents informed of weekly and monthly school events?
- What are the unique needs of the community we serve?
- How can parents be guided to support their children's academic and social success (e.g., homework, values)?
- Is there a consistency in reporting to parents?
- Does our reporting system need to be reassessed?
- How can the value of our policies be enhanced for parents (e.g., getting parent and staff input)?
- What directions should parent in-service take to best meet the needs of parents?
- How would our school look to a new parent?
- What process is employed when parents have an issue with a teacher? Does the staff understand how to diffuse conflict with a parent?
- What process is in place to handle parental concerns and questions about the school?
- How can we improve parent attendance at school events?
- How can schools use strong, informed parents to support the needs of families "at risk" (e.g., parents of children with learning disabilities)?
- How can parents support and encourage school spirit?
- How are parents informed of board wide issues (e.g., anti-racist policy)?
- How can we assist parents to develop new knowledge re: basic home-related issues such as providing adult computer courses, child management courses, and so on?

CHAPTER TWO

Basic Strategies

The Parents' Library

Schools might consider setting up a parents' library for a number of reasons. Books on parenting acknowledge that good parenting is a *learned skill*, often strengthened by reading. A library can also serve as a catalyst for informal meetings/discussions about parenting issues between parents or between parents and educators. The selection of books provides a focus for parent/teacher discussions, offering parents the opportunity to explore their parenting needs and teachers the opportunity to suggest books they have found helpful. At-risk parents can be drawn to parenting library information in a nonthreatening way, during local school team meetings, parent-teacher interviews, and so on.

Parents can benefit from libraries for a variety of reasons. Today's busy parents have less time to search out information on good parenting at local libraries and bookstores. Contemporary families have fewer extended family resources available to offer practical guidance, modelling, and support. Libraries also offer another legitimate reason for parents to visit the school.

A library promotes a caring climate that makes a "welcome" statement to the whole family. It values the role of the parents in developing strong students and represents a preventative model. The message to students is that both the parents and educators value reading and are working toward the same goal.

The Parents' Library might best be placed in a quiet corner within the office. This gives a strong message to parents about valuing their needs. It is the most open, accessible spot during most periods of the day. It also provides a space for support staff to include additional books, brochures, or magazine information (e.g., information from the school nurse).

To facilitate the lending of books, institute an honor system that assumes parents will voluntarily return the books. If parents feel trusted, the greater the chance that they will return the trust. The presence of the school secretary should jog the parents' memories to return the books. The school librarian could determine and post the length of time appropriate to keep the books (e.g., one book at a time for one month). A sign-out book should be made available.

The school community council could be approached for money to establish the library and for assistance in selecting/purchasing books they have found useful.

The books selected should represent the spectrum of issues parents and educators commonly encounter. Books might reflect the particular climate and curriculum that the school values. As an example, a school that advocates cooperative learning could share relevant guide books with parents. Schools representing families where English is a second language will need to meet their needs. Some literature might support parents by exploring positive, personal self-help issues. Others could outline the sequence of emotional, physical, cognitive, and social-developmental stages of children. Books published that outline places of interest to visit locally help parents to plan experiences for their children. Student social issues (e.g., smoking, drinking) may also be explored. In addition, some books may offer family cooperative learning activities (e.g., Family Math) while others serve as good resources (e.g., Roget's Thesaurus).

The style of books collected should reflect the family units of today — single parent families, shared parenting, and traditional family units. Selected literature should accomodate the literacy levels of the parents within the school community, and incorporate practical, informal formats. Humorous books are also easy to relate to and help parents see serious issues with less intensity. Schools might also offer books/author suggestions that can help parents to create personal family libraries.

A school parents' library could be expanded to include commercial education-related videos, school-made videos, parent magazines, films, community health newsletters, and small local newspapers.

A selection of educational resource materials for teachers will likely be available in the regular school library. Some books may be appropriate for both libraries, but not all. It's fair to recognize the similarities and differences between teacher education and parenting, as long as both are valued.

The Parents' Bulletin Board

One way to visibly help parents feel part of a school is to create a parents' bulletin board. If the board is in a high parent traffic area, more parents will have an opportunity to view it. A parent volunteer or educational assistant can be delegated the job of removing dated information and keeping it tidy. The board can include information on:

- upcoming school events involving parents (date, time, topic, location);
- upcoming school events for students;
- guiding principles of the school;
- newspaper articles pertinent to education/parenting;
- relevant community news — local library events, etc.;
- photographs of parent volunteers in recognition of their efforts in the school;
- requests for parental assistance;
- positive letters from parents and visitors;
- copies of school newsletters;
- newspaper articles about the school;
- relevant board policy information;
- parent-to-parent messages;
- examples of good student work;
- notice of upcoming P.D. days and the topics to be explored;
- after-four programs and heritage language schedules;
- lunch program and daycare notices, if applicable.

Parent Volunteers

Supportive parents who serve as volunteers and/or participants at meetings provide the school with invaluable endowments of time, energy, and talent. Without these gifts, crowded classrooms would lose the special nourishment that revitalizes both student and teacher alike.

As educators, we have observed through the years a few reasons why some parents hesitate to volunteer as supportive assistants. They are worth noting.

The parents may:
- have other overwhelming responsibilities;
- use English as a second language and don't feel competent to communicate freely;
- have poor self-esteem;
- feel unsure due to their own limited or different educational backgrounds;
- sense a school atmosphere that doesn't say "Welcome";
- reflect and dwell on their own unpleasant childhood experiences in school;
- have a child who seems unhappy at school or is having unsuccessful experiences;
- view education as the school's total responsibility.

One way a school can develop a more positive home/school partnership is to establish a small working committee of one or two teachers, an experienced volunteer, and a school administrator. After some discussions, the committee may wish to create two separate questionnaires, one for parents and one for staff, that invite feedback to the school about how each group values and views the roles of volunteers. The survey to the parents should make a strong, positive statement about how the volunteers are a welcome asset to the school. As followup, an informal presentation can be made to the Home and School Association by the committee. If their presentation is videotaped, it can model the school's views toward volunteers and be shown to new families transferring to the school. What a welcoming statement that would make!

Three possible questions for the Teacher's Survey could be:

1. How do you enlist the parent's help?

2. What are the three most important reasons you use parent volunteers?

3. If you are not presently using parent volunteers, would you like to use them next year? How could you use them?

Once the validity of parent volunteers has been established, their responsibilities must be determined. Parents working in schools should be involved in activities that directly impact children's learning. By giving parents these opportunities, we offer important messages: to children, that their parents value learning; to adults, that their expertise and experience are valued. It also serves to train parents in appropriate ways of supporting their own child's learning.

Parent volunteers hopefully will not always be mothers as fathers play a critical role as models for young children. Fathers may be able to come on a short-term basis to support a special project or teach strategy games. Encourage their participation.

Parent volunteers will help for varying lengths of time — once a week, for a special occasions, or on a regular basis. It is important to negotiate clearly what kind of commitment the parent is willing to make. If you are unsure of the potential unreliability or skills of a volunteer, tread slowly and gradually give them increasing responsibility.

Parents can. . .
- listen to children read individually;
- type stories ready to be published;
- help children do simple research;
- read to individual or small groups of children (material above their reading level);
- read stories (slowly) on tape to be stored at the listening center;
- accompany classes on excursions;
- become involved in activities and teach their own skills — teaching knitting, helping with the baseball team, working with the photography club, teaching computer skills, etc.;
- present personal stories to serve as models for careers;
- gather materials for a theme;
- run a book fair;
- write letters to other parents outlining an upcoming event or theme;
- teach children how to play games in the classroom;
- interact with children at a center;
- supervise a small group with a particular interest;
- work on a school yearbook, newsletter, etc.;
- serve as an audience for children's story ideas in all writing stages;
- help with the exchange of books for home reading;
- help students select books at the library;

- assist the school librarian;
- help families new to the school.

ESL parents can be an extremely valuable asset to school activities. Parents who speak two languages can . . .

- be a facilitator in writing — translate directions and written language, help students write in their first language, interpret students' writing in other languages, create dual language story books.
- be a facilitator in reading — read to children in their language, hear children read in their own language, help them with English script.
- become a buddy to a child or family from the same country — accompany the child on a tour of the school, encourage him/her to engage in classroom activities, answer questions the child may have about the school.
- contact families speaking the same language and welcome them to the neighborhood and the school.

Parent volunteers can also initiate and develop their own projects in conjunction with the school. In one school, environmentally conscious parents introduced a recycling program and created a wilderness garden with students. Parents know their talents best.

Many schools use parents to staff their safe arrival programs. Volunteer parents phone parents of students absent from school to determine if the children are legitimately absent. While this program does not deal directly with students, it does offer parents a specific role in the school where parents can work together purposefully and form new friendships. This program also provides opportunity for specific parents to take a meaningful leadership role.

Meaningful Memory

An inner-city parent once told Maureen that by watching teachers read and interact with children, she understood how to better relate to her child. Though the child had some difficulty reading, she was supportive of him and they read together each evening. Due to the demonstrations she had seen by teachers at school and the practice she had interacting with other students, the mother was better prepared to positively handle her son. Her work as a parent volunteer directly impacted her relationship with her child and hopefully his future academic success.

Wouldn't it be great if. . .

the parents presence in the school would not only benefit children, but provide an opportunity for open, honest dialogue about educational issues between parents and teachers. Informal discussion allows both parents and teachers a chance to clear up misunderstandings and misinformation.

parents were in-serviced prior to working in schools to help orient and train them to work most effectively with students, as well as help them to understand the dynamics of a particular school and education in general.

Parent Workshops

"Parents of teachers who build parent involvement (parent workshops) into their regular teaching practice were more aware of teachers' efforts, received more ideas from teachers, knew more about their child's instructional program, and rated the teachers higher in interpersonal skills and overall teaching quality."

Joyce L. Epstein, Elementary School Journal

If schools are to empower parents to truly impact students' learning, we need to take the initiative to provide parent education. Educators have the resources, leadership personnel, and teaching backgrounds to welcome parents into our teaching/learning environment. It takes extra energy to involve parents in shared experiences with educators, but the payback to educators, parents, and students is well worth the effort. If parent workshops are considered a key component in building student success then schools must problem solve around time management and workshop structure.

Parent Workshops: Some Considerations

Schools need to look carefully at teaching demands and prioritize items parents need to understand in order to best affect student outcomes. Numerous workshops for parents each year do not need to be offered. Decide what information is most important for parents to receive and what issues are most critical to the school. If teams of teachers are formed, the workload is shared and so are ideas. Consultants and other outside resource personnel can help plan, provide current information, and copresent at the workshop. Presenters will also require release time to plan. Possible compensation time for the extra hours of work should be considered. Some Boards of Education will support workshops through Continuing Education Departments.

Administrators can contribute support to parent workshops by playing an active, supportive role in planning and presenting at parent workshops. They can provide a small school budget to be set aside for refreshments, materials, and so on. Administrators can also consider presenting an in-service to assist educators working with parents. A P.D. day might be used to support this. In addition, administrators can facilitate the sharing of successful in-service models from other schools.

The most successful parent afternoons or evenings are informal gatherings where parents have time to talk and listen to one another. Meetings for parents can be planned/organized using the same interactive, dynamic, problem solving processes used with students. Educators might also create an active role for parents in the presentation. An evaluation or reflection by parents and teachers at the end of a workshop can offer objective feedback for future events.

Educators are not always experts and should not present themselves as such. Like others, we are continually learning and experimenting as we cope with changing times. Taking risks and making mistakes are necessary and inevitable in growth. We should be open-minded about sharing our reasoning, thinking, beliefs, and experiences with parents.

Parent in-service should reflect the current needs and concerns of educators, parents, or students. As an example, based on the needs of her at-risk readers, one educator held a parent workshop on basic reading strategies and ways parents could support and encourage reading.

A successful parent workshop should be planned using the same sound teaching/learning principles that we use with students. It should incorporate the same kind of active, engaging experiences that teachers are offered at their in-service meetings.

We can no longer expect parents (or students) to listen for hours and remain stimulated and enthusiastic.

A workshop might include:

- parents and teachers discussing an issue and possible solutions, for example, working together to create better home/school communications, solving school conflicts, etc.;
- parents creating questions and sharing experiences with other parents. This serves as an opportunity for parents to recognize and relate to their needs, for example, understanding the school evaluation system.

Parents, in groups, might generate ten questions about education in general and the school specifically. Through creative problem solving and the application of their knowledge and observation, parents attempt to answer the questions. Those questions that remain unanswered could be addressed during the next meeting by educators knowledgeable in the area. Sample questions could be:

Do children learn to read in kindergarten?
How do you teach reading?
Can we help our child in spelling at home?
What are your after-school programs?
How and when do you report to parents?

Parents should have the opportunity to observe educators as they demonstrate teaching practices, strategies, and behaviors so that they can better understand their child's educational experiences. Parents should also have time to practice the strategies in class in order to use them at home.

The meeting should resemble a casual gathering of friends, incorporating informal invitations, a seating arrangement that encourages interaction, and refreshments that are available throughout the workshop. Use a room in the school that is conducive to this type of meeting. Hopefully, the comfort level between teachers and parents will increase.

Some schools develop a "make and take" where parents copy/create learning tools to use with their children. Simple games and activities can be developed or reproduced by parents. This creates a less intimidating atmosphere, as well as providing an opportunity for parents and teachers to chat comfortably about the use of the games.

Parents might:

- copy bingo-style games that reinforce the use of common words;
- create concentration/matching games using words and pictures;
- develop sets of compound words for matching games (e.g., snow man);
- tape a favorite story to let children/read listen to at home;
- make a cumulative cooperative group story to be taken home for children to finish and bring back;
- create and publish a book sharing a childhood experience. This book can be shared at home before being placed in the class library;
- develop a cooperative list of their childrens' favorite books.

Note:
Translators and babysitters may be needed by some parents. A visible agenda or menu helps parents to know the direction the evening will take.

Planning the Workshop

Meet with educators involved and select a date that is acceptable for all groups. Avoid holding workshops on religious holidays of any group within the school. Once you have obtained your permit to use the school after hours, draw up a friendly invitation to parents, identifying the time, date, and nature of the workshop. Give parents lots of advance warning. Once these details have been taken care, coordinate and delegate tasks for the workshop. Consider the objective and topic of the workshop and go to it!

Format

This format should create positive feelings for both parents and teacher(s).

1. *Workshop Objective*

2. Personal Experience/Opener

Listening to the experiences of another relaxes parents, fills some of the social needs, and creates a positive working climate. As well, it begins to focus the group around the topic of the evening. An example of an opener might be related to a workshop around reading. You might ask parents, in pairs, to introduce themselves and briefly talk about one of their child's favorite story books. Parents change pairs so they can meet others in the workshop. Limit the time of this introduction activity to ten minutes.

3. Modeling, Direct Instruction, Guided Practice, Creative Problem Solving, or Generating Questions

At this point, parents may be exposed to a short, focussed "text" about an educational issue, a movie, a short article, or a guest speaker. Parents discuss, in large or small groups, the implications and applications as it relates to their child.

Educators might model learning strategies or practices parents might use with their children or that promote understanding of the learning process. Parents may work individually, in pairs, or in small groups to practice a strategy before they use it with their own children.

Educators might present a community/school issue. Parents and educators, in small groups, brainstorm possible solutions and present their ideas. As a whole group, the participants select the most suitable solutions and plan their implementation.

4. Reflection, Evaluation, and Independent Application

Each workshop should include a shared reflection/evaluation component that includes both parents and teachers. This information helps to provide knowledge for future planning. Independent application refers to parents relating/practicing a strategy, philosophy, or information within their own families. Parents and teachers should celebrate the efforts they made as involved and caring partners, and recognize the important messages they offer students about willingness to learn at any age, and about valuing the contributions of others.

Suggested Workshop Topics

A. Curriculum Topics

Cooperative/Collaborative Learning
Drama
Values
Language (e.g., Writing Workshop)
Make & Take (parent-created activities, games for use at home)
Evaluation
Goal Setting
Research and Projects
Multi-age Grouping
Strategic Planning for Parents
Problem Solving/Posing Questions
Studying and Homework
Integrated Themes
Thinking Strategies
Stages of Reading and Writing
Teaching Spelling
Reading Aloud
Reading Strategies
Storytelling
Responding to Stories
Media Literacy
Ways Children Record Information and Ideas
A Typical Day
Games — Commercial/Handmade
Writing Workshop
Family Math
Language Partners
The Stages of Spelling
What to Do with Your Children During the Summer
Anti-Racist Education/Identifying Bias

B. Culmination of a Theme (Classroom or School-wide)

Parents provide an audience for student learning.

C. Parent Support

How to Talk to Your Kids About . . .
Sexuality/Smoking/Drinking/Drugs
Expectations/Manners/Setting Limits
Rights and Responsibilities
Peer Pressure/Making Choices
Handling Money
Conflict Resolution
Celebrating Success
Violence/Streetproofing
Television

Unintentionally, senior/secondary educators and older students sometimes give parents the message that they should not play a direct role in education. Students can see parent involvement as a threat to their growing independence while educators, working with rotary classes, lack time to deal with the many families involved.

The parents of some students continue to play a strong, supportive role with the home serving as the arena. Concerned parents provide a positive climate for homework, monitor social relationships, and negotiate adolescent issues as they develop.

Parents can develop informal support groups and meet at schools to discuss relevant teenage issues. These groups offer parents opportunities to share problems and possible solutions with one another. An informal network helps parents of adolescents renew acquaintances and lend support.

A Model for Values Studies

Stage One

A mutual concern between the home and school executive and the principal lead to the formation of a committee to study values within the school and family. Due to staff time constraints, a trio of parents research relevant information. The parents are invited to report their findings to a staff workshop on a P.D. day. A discussion ensues in which both parents and teachers reach a consensus as to the meaning of values as they apply to the school. The parent committee reports to the home and school association as well.

Stage Two

Each class is involved in a discussion as to what values mean to them. Two representatives from each class are selected to join other student representatives. They draw up a collaborative chart that details students' rights and responsibilities at the school.

Stage Three

At the "Meet the Teacher Night" in the fall, the process and the chart are shared with the parents. In small groups, parents discuss the implications for their children and themselves, and decide how they might take ownership of this within their homes.

Meaningful Memories

At one school, a reception center for ESL parents representing fifty-five language groups, parents met to learn about the school and the community. In language groups (with translators when required) or in heterogeneous groups, parents met in small groups and generated educational questions they wanted answered. Parent "reporters" presented the questions to the whole group. Teachers accepted the responsibility for gathering information and presenting it to the parents during a series of evenings. Answers to the questions were given through various media sources, for example, quest speakers and printed material from various community organizations.

Miriam, a kindergarten teacher, became alarmed at the negative physical interaction among her students as they roleplayed television superheroes. She sent a letter home to the parents asking them to observe their children's television choices over a two-week period. After two weeks, parents were invited to the school to discuss and problem solve these concerns. The outcome was that parents became more aware of the need to monitor children's television viewing more frequently and convert negative play into more positive situations. Miriam saw the workshop as a worthwhile, informal way to address a pressing need. Parents realized that other families had the same concern.

At another school, there was a school-wide initiative where teachers received drama in-service in preparation for a week-long drama experience for students. A parent in-service was planned to help parents understand the value of drama experiences in the curriculum. Debbie, a drama coordinator agreed to provide real drama experiences for parents. Initially she expected a maximum of twenty parents to participate. However, she coped with seventy parents working in teams, playing drama games, roleplaying, and speaking numerous languages. It was a highly successful event full of boisterous, laughing parents, fully engaged in the learning process.

At a cooperative learning parent workshop, an immigrant parent schooled in a very different system, sat down, looked at Maureen and asked, "When is the next meeting for parents?" Obviously the workshop format had met some of his needs.

Lynn, a teacher, invited parents to her class at the end of each classroom theme. At the culmination of a unit on "heroes and heroines" each of the students painted a large head of their chosen hero and dressed in role. Parents moved throughout the room conversing with "Helen Keller", "Golda Meyer", "Norman Bethune", etc. Students, talking in role, used their knowledge and imagination to develop their characters as they interacted with parents.

At the end of a unit on law and government, parents formed a jury and heard defendants, lawyers, judges, witnesses, and prosecutors develop their legal cases. The trial offered children a meaningful focus for their learning, and the decision of the jury created anticipation during the evening.

From a Parent

On February 16th, in the evening, I wanted to stay home. It had been a long day, there was housework to do and it was very cold outside. But we parents had been invited to an educational meeting at the school and I had heard that the students of parents who show an interest do better at school. So I went to school. It was my best evening in a long time. We laughed, we learned and I think every parent there was glad they came.

Noreen Hardwick, the guest speaker, teaches teachers how to make cooperative learning fun for our children. She had us adults working and having fun together in groups of people who hadn't known each other before. This made me feel a lot better about my son getting involved and making friends at school. With her methods, you couldn't stay quiet because every idea was important.

What impressed me the most was when a group wrote a story in their own language and read it to all of us. Nobody except that group knew what was being said, but everyone was quiet and really listened to the reader. The words sounded nice and we all knew it was a happy story, even though we couldn't understand a word. At that time, I wished more than anything I knew the language.

Wouldn't it be great if. . .

the workshops developed into collaborative experiences where teachers and parents genuinely impacted and influenced one another's growth.

CHAPTER THREE

Avenues of Communication

Welcoming Letters

One way a classroom teacher can build positive parent relationships is to send a welcoming letter to his/her future students during the summer. Students are thrilled with this personal letter from their teacher while their parents view this as a thoughtful attempt at outreach.

At one school, teachers interested in sending a summer letter received a computerized list of all potential students and their addresses as of the end of June. During the summer, teachers personalized the style of their letters. One teacher wrote short messages on postcards bought on a trip he took during the summer vacation. Another made a game of the letters. Each student who brought his/her letter on the first day of school received a small treat. These letters became a starting point for team building during September. Other teachers wrote a general, newsy note and xeroxed copies. They filled in the student's names with a thin black marker to personalize each letter. The exercise took a maximum of two hours; the effect was well worth the time.

A sample letter might look like this:

Dear _____,

I am really looking forward to meeting you in September. We will be involved in some very exciting learning during the year. I have planned a class trip to the Science Center where we can explore science in our world. I'm sure you will also enjoy some of the science experiments we will do in our classroom.

I hope you're enjoying your summer, visiting places around our neighborhood and beyond. I also hope you're reading a book or two and taking part in some of the programs at our local library. We like to read in our classroom, so if you have some books you've really enjoyed, please tell us about them in September.

I'm enjoying my holiday, too. I took a course for teachers about reading, and I'm also thinking about interesting ideas for our class.

See you on September 5th.

Yours truly,

Mrs. Botrie

Welcoming Procedures

We're all familiar with this scene. A new family enters the school. Through trial and error, they make their way to the office. Family members — father, mother, children — peek around the corner. The administrative assistant, typist, and principal are deep in conversation over a school issue. The family quietly enters the office and sits on a bench while the office administrative group continues its conversation. The family becomes increasingly uncomfortable. The school secretary is involved elsewhere.

Would you feel welcome? Let's replay this scenario.

A new family enters the school and follows signs (posted in all necessary languages) to the office door. Although the administrative assistant, typist, and principal are deep in conversation over a school issue, they pause and smile. The secretary says, ''As soon as we're finished here we'll be pleased to help you.'' The family responds positively and looks forward to having their needs met.

There are many ways schools offer an inviting message to new families — personal interaction with staff, welcoming structures, and the physical appearance of the school.

The look of the school reflects the importance placed on a welcoming appearance; an attractive school is usually perceived by visitors to be friendly. Welcome and direction signs strategically posted throughout the school reassure families that that their presence is positively received. A comfortable reception area for parents and visitors can provide written information about the school or a video on the topic. Adult chairs in the office offer parents an appropriate place to sit versus punitive benches that lack comfort, among other things.

The staff that families meet throughout the school can create an inviting feeling. Office staff can be encouraged to welcome all visitors warmly and politely. Teachers and other school staff members recognize their roles in developing a welcoming climate in the school. Schools can also determine times when the principal is available to meet with parents, making sure these are clearly posted.

Structures can be put in place to welcome families and newcomers. A school "buddy" system can link new students with those familiar with the school so that newcomers acclimatize more easily. Each class can be invited to design their own welcoming procedures to integrate new students into the school, for example, welcoming letters to parents, packages of materials for students, and manipulatives and games to help students feel comfortable. Clear, precise written information should be provided to answer parents' queries about the lunchroom program, daycare programs, after four activities, and so on.

Schools can provide easy student and teacher access to phones. Students should know that the school supports student/parent communication during the school day. If a telephone is placed on an office counter, it's accessible to students without disrupting the office. Its use can be monitored. Phoning parents provides flexibility and a "safety net" for children. If phones are installed on each floor of the school, teachers can contact parents with a minimum of fuss and delay.

Wouldn't it be great if. . .

families could be "twinned" to create a family support network. Willing families could offer their names as contacts for new families. When contacted, the established families could offer an informal tie with the neighborhood, answering questions, outlining community resources, and providing a personalized welcome.

Meet the Teacher (Creature) Night

"Of all the things that count, nothing is as important as the people in the process. Teaching machines, micro-computers, programmed materials and other technological advances may have an important place in education, but they cannot substitute for human relationships."

William Purkey, Inviting School Success

Mention an upcoming "Meet the Teacher Night" at an early fall staff meeting and most teachers begin to squirm uncomfortably. A few outwardly groan. It's an evening in which teachers seem to feel targeted by parental expectations they cannot fulfill so early in the school year. However, it is inevitable that every parent's first concern is his/her own child (and rightly so). Parents often want to restructure the evening into individual parent interviews, making the teacher ill at ease. As a result, neither adult partner is satisfied.

A renaming and restructuring of the evening should be considered if it is to continue at this time of year. Schools might consider a broader focus with a name such as T.E.A.M.S. Night (Together Everyone Achieves More Success), S.C.H.O.O.L. Night (School Curriculum Has Objectives Of Learning), or W.E.L.C.O.M.E. (We Enjoy Learning, Caring, Opportunity, and Meaningful Education) or "Get To Know Your School" Night. Appealing invitations will encourage parents to come.

Consider these models of parent evenings:

An evening is organized around a draft of an overall school focus, such as values and guiding principles. Teachers and parents, in small groups, discuss a specific issue, its applications and implications within the home, the community, and the school. The principal explains the implications of the development of this initiative to the audience of educators and parents (children, if invited). Small groups then collaborate on the direction of the initiative within the school. Finally, creative solutions/ideas/comments are shared with the large group.

or

The principal shares with the entire audience the vision/guiding principles, expectations, directions, or initiatives for the upcoming year. Following this, teachers meet by grade division with parents in different areas of the school. Prior to the evening, teachers meet to identify programming common to all classes. Each teacher briefly shows examples of work samples and explains a small portion of the program, for example, Home Reading programs, and writing folders. Parents meet with one or two teachers in small groups and share questions about programming.

or

Invite children and parents to the school. Encourage each family to tour all the rooms associated with the child's growth (e.g., library, gym). The child takes the leadership role and explains through his/her eyes the significance of each room as it relates to his/her learning. We see this informal, uncomplicated model as a powerful partnership. It gives students an opportunity to summarize and clarify their understanding of school to a supportive audience.

or

If children are unable to participate in the evening, teachers might invite all parents visiting the room to write a message on a large piece of paper. Comments from visitors should be positive and encouraging, reflecting what parents observed about the classroom. Parents can also leave individual messages for their children. The parents' personal statements could be left up and referred to during the year.

Meaningful Memory

Inner-city parents can be more hesitant to attend parent meetings. At Queen Victoria, the goal was to have every parent come to visit the school early in the fall. Each family was telephoned to encourage them to attend. Parent response to the personal phone invitations was strong.

Wouldn't it be great if . . .

schools could develop such an initial climate of trust early in the year that the positive impact influenced parent/teacher relations for the rest of the year?

Open House

Education Week and Open House Evenings can provide a framework for parent education and meaningful interaction between parents and staff. Before an Open House, schools might explore ways to present their philosophy, offer examples of their students' development and progress, and display print and nonprint resources throughout the school.

To foster parents' understanding of the underlying currents of education, teachers might present their curriculum in a variety of formats. Learning stations could be set up in each classroom. Parents might try activities at each station that reflect different curriculum areas. Stations should reflect the kinds of books, computer programs, manipulatives, and materials their children will handle during the year. An alternative is for students to model typical learning activities for their parents. Parents can be offered demonstrations of computer programs, science experiments, music, novels or big books, drama activities, published books, problem solving, poetry reading, storytelling, and so on. Stagger the demonstration times so parents can visit many spots.

During another evening, students could be invited to act as guides for their families as they move throughout the school. On the invitation, ask parents to question their child about his/her learning as they tour the school. This offers students an opportunity to "retell" their educational experiences and reflect on their learning. Prior to the evening, students might consider through writing or discussion what they should tell their parents about their school. Staff might also display in the gym or other large space examples illustrating the development of children's writing and stages of reading. Staff can explain the progression to parents.

Education Week/Open House evenings can also serve as a culmination for a school-wide theme. All classes can reflect on one learning focus for parents to enjoy. Student guides can explain their models, projects, writing, and art that explore the theme. Teachers can encourage parents to visit all classrooms by providing a questionnaire that asks families to find answers to questions about the theme in each classroom. Completed questionnaires could be submitted for a lucky draw at the close of the evening. Consider ways parents might be involved in the school-wide theme, for example, dressing up to reflect the theme, baking appropriate foods at home, and so on. A festive, celebratory mood can be created.

These evenings offer an opportunity to focus on parent involvement in schools. Staff can recruit new parent volunteers and honor parents who currently work in the school. Photographs and captions outlining parent contributions draw attention from both parents and children. This is also a good time to publicize upcoming events offered in the school. A Parents' Corner can be created in each classroom. It might house statements of philosophy, a student-of-the-week display, classroom newsletters, handouts, or letters for parents to take home. As parents visit classrooms, they could receive relevant newspaper and magazine articles, view examples of students' work reflective of the stages of development, browse through current curriculum guides, and perhaps borrow an educational book.

Parent Interviews

Inner-city parents often feel intimidated when they're invited to visit the school, perhaps due to past experience. Yet the importance of parents showing interest in their child's school progress cannot be underestimated. In an effort to help parents feel more comfortable and confident during parent interviews, the form on the next page was sent home with interview times. Parents were encouraged to read the interview guidelines in advance. Should you wish, these guidelines can be copied and given to parents. The intent was to create a comfort level, and to increase their personal understanding and knowledge of the interview process.

These questions and comments helped parents and teachers participate more equally in the education process. The language used reflected English proficiency of some of the parents. Valuing their importance is implicit.

Parent/Teacher Interviews: How Do They Help?

You can get to know the person your child spends a large part of the day with.

You can share information and plan ways to help your child do the best s/he can in school.

Your child sees that you and the teacher think that what s/he does at school is important.

You can find out how well your child is learning and working with others.

Some things you may like to share with the teacher:

- your child's feelings about school;
- the activities your child likes to do at home or in the community;
- your child's reactions to home rules;
- your child's relationship with other family members;
- your child's relationship with other children in the neighborhood;
- health problems of your child that the teacher should know about.

Some things you may want to ask the teacher:

Is my child making progress in the classroom?
Does my child have good work habits?
Does my child accept responsibility for his/her work and jobs?
How does my child get along with other children/adults in the classroom and in the playground?
Does my child behave appropriately and arrive on time?
What things does my child enjoy or show interest in at school?
What things does my child do well and what things does s/he need help with?

The authors would like to acknowledge the contribution of Glenys McCreath to the development of this form.

During interviews, parents and teachers were encouraged to collaborate in developing goals. Parents' and teachers' plans of action grew out of students' strengths and areas of concern. A brief written outline for parents and teachers served as a reminder of their discussion throughout the term.

Reporting

"We have learned that parents want to be treated as equal partners, and that the majority of them will help their children if we provide them with the information they need."

Carole Kennedy, Parent Involvement: It Takes Pep

When we attended elementary school, each report card that arrived home was carefully scrutinized for the A, B, C, and D gradings that it contained. Within each classroom, the students were compared to one another, usually in relation to isolated written tests addressing similarly isolated skills. Little was learned about how the individual student was growing and developing.

Today, educators are struggling to develop new methods of assessment that reflect children's personal growth throughout their school experience, as well as developing reporting methods to parents that are more interactive. As we examine our assessment and reporting methods, we might consider the issues parents, children, and educators have raised around reporting.

Parents feel schools do not share concerns early enough in the school year and in the child's school experience. As well, they feel educators don't always offer specific ways parents can support their child's learning. Our traditional report cards can be jargon-filled, impersonal, inconsistent, and uninformative. Report cards offer little concrete data about their child's growth over a period of time.

Many schools are struggling with the issues around traditional report cards and reporting procedures. Teachers feel such reporting does not reflect the way we teach today, for example: detailing results of goal setting by teachers and students, collaborative work, student ownership, continual evaluation of process and product, and so on. Report cards do not always demonstrate what a student knows, his/her learning process, daily progress, needs, and experiences. Traditional report cards can be seen as irrelevant in today's teaching-learning process, and as having little real influence in supporting children's growth. Given those failings, it is not illogical that report cards are often viewed as a waste of teachers' time.

Students have their own concerns around traditional report cards and reporting procedures. Report cards, as stated, do not always relate to students' personal development, their classroom experiences, and the way they learn. Students' strengths and areas of concern are not clearly revealed as traditional report cards leave little room for student self-evaluation, comments, and reactions about their learning. The inclusion of educational jargon clouds the relevance of the report and makes interpretation difficult for students. Also, traditional reporting comments on what has passed, not on goal setting and steps students can take to improve their performance.

Report cards can also be intimidating because of the anxiety aroused by sharing student progress with parents. Unless you are a perfect student there are negative feelings around report cards. Finally, traditional parent-teacher interviews intimate that learning is only the business of parents and teachers, excluding the student's voice and rightful role in the interview.

We feel that there are some basic principles around assessment and reporting that should shape a school's reporting policy. These are:

1. *Students should be part of the parent/teacher conference.*

   By inviting young children to the meeting, parents and teachers provide positive reinforcement regarding the child's education. Older children present at a conference have an opportunity to dialogue with both parties about their education and their perception of the learning process. They are the ones who must initiate and process any necessary changes.

2. *Both parents should be invited to the conference.*

   Each parent has a unique relationship with his/her child. If the conference is seen as geared toward mothers, the important link of the father will not be utilized. If there is shared custody of a child, it is imperative that the school inform all significant adults about conferences and other opportunities to communicate.

3. *A parent/teacher conference is a tremendous opportunity for teachers to congratulate parents.*

Parents, like teachers, need positive reinforcement about their skills as parents. If teachers can identify and share with all parents that they are doing a good job, parents will be pleased. This response will carry over to their child. As teachers, we need to find the good in all parents and share it with them. It is the most fragile parents who need the most support.

4. *Ask students to fill in their own separate report card.*

If the task is presented as though students have the most knowledge about their attitudes, work habits, and academic success they can reflect about themselves within the context of school. Students consider their own performance as a learner and fill in the report as if they were evaluating themselves. This report card is shared at the conference with the family. It offers an opportunity for students to assess both strengths and concerns prior to the meeting. During the meeting it provides concrete evidence of the perspective of both teacher and student. Filling out a report card is also a valid, reflective, relevant expository writing experience for students.

5. *Willing teachers might ask their students to assess them.*

When students fill out a report on teachers it offers a window into the eyes of the students. This form of student assessment encourages teacher reflection.

Many schools are moving to oral reporting during the first term. Schools might consider the impact of no written report card. Parents are then left with an eight-month gap (between June of one school year and February of the next) where there is no written evaluation. It is important for educators and parents to recognize that a written report card can be used as a reference point long after an interview has taken place. Placing a report card on the 'fridge serves as a focus for celebration. Parents can continually reinforce student successes and reflect on needs. Friends and relatives also have an opportunity to engage in a celebration. The report card serves as a written reminder of goals that can be set, and students can use a written report to focus their directions. Even a poorly designed report card can serve as a learning tool by parents if they use it toward this end. There is still a place for both kinds of reporting.

Another potential problem with oral report cards is the distortions they can invite. Each parent, following the interview, will take away his/her interpretation and perspective of the interview, having selectively heard what they already believe to be true about their child (either positive or negative). A parent's interpretation may then be offered to others, rather than the real information shared at an interview.

A concern for teachers is that some information is inappropriate for a child to hear. If this is the case, the child should be asked to step outside during this part of the conference.

We might consider spending our energy developing more informative, frequent, and personalized ways of reporting. A Home School Connection book, sent weekly or even monthly to parents, shares relevant comments about a child's work and attitude during that period. As well, the book asks parents for support in particular areas. Students and parents have an opportunity to include their written concerns and viewpoints. In schools where such a book has been used, parent feedback has been very positive.

In the example below, the parents of Thomas are provided with information about their son's week at school, while Thomas can express his joy at receiving a good report.

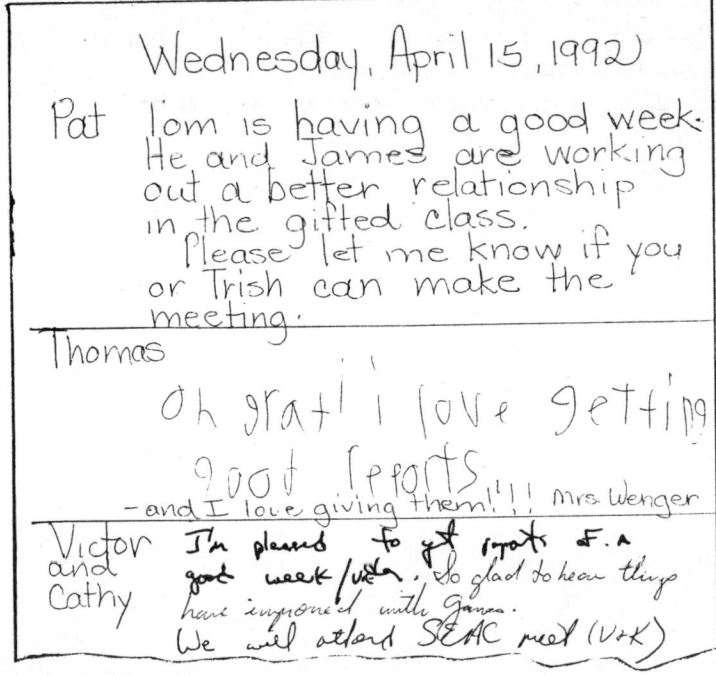

Wednesday, April 15, 1992)

Pat   Tom is having a good week. He and James are working out a better relationship in the gifted class.
Please let me know if you or Trish can make the meeting.

Thomas   Oh grat! i love getting good reports!!
— and I love giving them!!!! Mrs. Wenger

Victor and Cathy   I'm pleased to get reports of a good week/visit. So glad to hear things have improved with James.
We will attend SEAC meet (V+K)

During the conference, parents need to have an equal voice and an opportunity to report their observations of their child's learning during the previous term. A form letter could be distributed, inviting parents to comment on their perception of their child's growth during the last term. This feedback includes parent perspectives at home and broadens information available on the child.

Parents, students, and teachers should collaborate during an interview to develop goals. A brief written outline for parents and teachers could serve as a reminder of the discussion throughout the term. A copy for parents and students would remind them of their responsibilities and focus during the term. The next meeting of parents, students, and teachers should monitor and evaluate progress made toward the goals.

A possible model when working with individual parents and a teacher, or groups of parents and teachers might be:

Identification of the Problem
Discussion about the parameters of the problem
(i.e., brainstorming all possible solutions)
Decisions about what the parents might do
Decisions about what the teachers might do
Decisions about how the problem will be monitored and evaluated in a collaborative mode

These decisions have to be made by each party, not imposed by one group on another. Parent/teacher relationships cannot become a fight for control and power as this is not beneficial to the students. It is important to realize that in such a situation no side will "win".

Wouldn't it be great if . . .

a student was assured by their local board that s/he would be a partner in the reporting/conference process from kindergarten to the end of high school.

Shared Written Communication (Using the School Binder)

General written communications are as much of a challenge to the school as they are to the parents who receive them. From the school office and teachers' perspectives, it seems as if paper work is scattered about like a constant flurry of snowflakes.

At school, these questions often pervade the atmosphere of the principal's office. "What information needs to go home and why?" "When should it go home, how often, and to whom? We know that with shared parenting a fact of life, notices often arrive at the first home but seldom at the second.

No one in the educational field would question the value of shared communication between school and home. However, our environmental global dilemma demands effective solutions of saving, distributing, and storing paper. As parents and teachers, we agreed that within our own homes, valuable school flyers were regularly misplaced and inadvertently thrown out. Certainly, most families have bulletin boards to keep current schedules, but may not accommodate all types of information. Parents who are inundated with school information still claim they don't understand what is being taught, why, and how.

Brainstorming led to the following solution. If possible, have your home and school community association raise funds to purchase three-ring binders for each family (and educator) within the school. A creative challenge could then go out to the students to design an appropriate logo and/or name for the binders. All notices from the school that are meant to be kept could be prepunched and identified before being sent home. In essence, the binder becomes a school handbook. As the school evolves, new directions and emphases could be added, and outdated information deleted.

Consider storing the following school items:

- school expectations and behavior/values codes;
- information on the School Community Council, parent volunteers, and research statements on parent involvement;
- information on school programs (e.g., the writing process, partners in action) following parent in-service;
- short, pertinent articles on learning that support the school's beliefs;

- information on how parents can support their child at home —
    organizational strategies,
    support programs like Family Math,
    Language Partners,
    Home Reading,
    helping with homework,
    value of daily experiences, etc.;
- list of local outings and places to visit (if applicable, mention no charge time/days);
- listing of all current parent volunteers;
- positive "how-to" advice about parenting;
- suggested reading list of parenting books or magazines;
- notes on health issues, policies, and nurse availability;
- report card/interview/placement information;
- papers and report cards regarding exceptional children;
- daycare, lunch, or after school program outlines, as well as policies, fee structure, and contact people;
- school and community phone numbers — nurse, office, safe arrival, sports, drama, music, French program, news;
- annual special events with tentative dates (e.g., graduation, concerts, etc.);
- P.D. days and report card interview dates;
- school/class excursions planned with dates;
- "P.R." to develop a positive image of the school (e.g., news articles);
- monthly newsletters;
- personal communication from teachers (e.g. welcoming letters);
- samples of children's best work;
- list of suggested commercial games and computer programs;
- list of special school teams and clubs;
- book list of favorite authors for particular ages;
- local library timetable and permanent events.

The list goes on. Each school's guidebook will reflect their particular emphasis while each family binder can be re-evaluated at summer's end in preparation for the next school year. In cooperative parenting situations where the student has two homes, the binder can be an important link between his/her three worlds.

When different services in the school are invited to make a brief statement for the handbook, the people involved have a chance to think and talk about the service they provide. This opportunity to discuss together can only be beneficial.

A final suggestion . . . use a special colored paper to denote staff forms that should be included in their handbooks through-out the year.

Wouldn't it be great if . . .

each Board of Education provided home/school binders as a part of the regular school issue of supplies. What a positive supportive statement this would make in promoting the home/school connection.

Newsletters

One of the most productive ways to enrich interaction between home and school is to develop a monthly newsletter. Each person can participate in a manner that maximizes his/her creative talents.

One method that has proven successful is the formation of a three-parent committee that collects, collates, and edits information from classrooms, sports teams, music/drama groups, and after school programs. Stories are submitted by students, small groups, parents, families, and professional staff. The home/school association and the daycare post reminders about upcoming special events and regular meetings. The newsletter is an unequalled link that enables all parents to remain well-informed about school events and talent.

Consider placing the names of noncustodial parents on a mailing list so that they, too, will become informed partners in education.

Decide on these basic questions.
• How often should you publish?
• Who will do what?
• Where will the funds for paper, etc. come from?
• How will contributions be collected? from each class? from interested classes?
• What kinds of events will be covered?
• How much responsibility can students reasonably be asked to take? (The newsletter might be the pet project of one class.)

- What is the easiest way to distribute finished newsletters?
- How are we informing the rest of the staff about these decisions?
- How much school-wide commitment is there for a newsletter? (The answer to this question helps a committee decide on what a reasonable workload for other teachers might be.)
- What are the English literacy levels of the families reading the newsletter? (This information will assist the committee in choosing an appropriate style.)

One school had a computer printout of all the students who were the oldest in their family. Newsletters, along with a xeroxed sheet of the printout, were sent to each classroom. This saved paper and duplication of service. Another school that instituted this policy found the newsletters to be so popular that each child, regardless of his/her position in the family, wanted to take one home. The school reverted to the former policy of giving each child his/her personal copy.

Newsletters can be used as a text for learning. In one class, students use the newsletters as they would any effective shared experience. Initially, the teacher models excitement and interest on receiving the newsletter. Using her lead, students demonstrate the same behaviors — reading the newsletter, helping one another read, exchanging comments about the text, listening to others — being totally involved with print. If circumstances arise that delay use of the newsletter in the classroom, keep them for use at a more convenient date. Students will still find them of interest.

Ask parents to write articles for the newsletter. They might pose questions and make suggestions about home issues in a Parents' Corner. Parents might also function as writers and reviewers, reporting on a parents' night, workshops, and so on. Such reporting of educational events helps everyone respect the partnership between home and school.

Parents often become concerned when students' first draft writing is published without corrections. Some parents become anxious with what they perceive as a lack of spelling skills, and fail to recognize the age of the writers. If you think unedited work might cause this response, create a policy that all creative writing articles must be edited for spelling and style, or add a statement at the bottom of each newsletter explaining that the work is a first draft. An issue containing draft pieces can serve as a focus for discussion about what parents infer when they see students' work. An articulated school vision can increase parents' understanding of child development and stages of learning.

Newsletters asking for parents' opinions on school issues can be very informative to educators, and offer parents another voice in the school. Each newsletter might include a tear-off section and one question about education, for example:

- Do you understand the way spelling is being taught in our school?
- How can the school organize our parent interview nights to better service you?
- Do you believe your children enjoy our school?
- What kind of comments do your children offer about their learning?
- Which events at the school did you feel were most worthwhile this year?
- Should the school consider offering hot lunches? If so, how would you be willing to pay?

Even a minimal response rate offers schools a window into parents' viewpoints, needs, and suggestions for improvements. It also makes parents feel like contributors to the decisions made at their school. Responses should be shared with appropriate parties, for example: the home and school association, specific committees, and administration.

As well as containing local school news, the newsletter can be used to inform parents about educational issues. Up to eight lines of educational articles can be copied. Parents who wish to read the rest of the article(s) can submit a tear-off section requesting the entire article. In respecting parent's individual needs and interests, we are encouraging them to become more involved in education. Even if no one requests the articles, it is important that they be offered.

A problem with newsletters is that they can be treated as another piece of junk mail to be discarded without first being read. If the newsletter is visually attractive with lots of school photos and student drawings, parent interest is captured quickly.

If a school's parent clientele tends to be nonreaders of English, photographs or drawings can form the basis of the newsletter. Add a short caption under each picture; bear in mind that too much print is formidable. Keep a school camera handy and loaded to capture meaningful events at the school. You'll find that there numerous camera-worthy opportunities.

Acknowledge ESL parents and students by:

- translating general statements like the principal's message, homework tips, and notes on values education in languages that reflect the population of the school.
- including student writing in other languages.
- asking bilingual parent volunteers to talk with ESL students about the articles in the newsletter.

— In addition, try:

- keeping it simple. Create a format. Try not to impose themes or tight control of content. Each person needs to feel free to write what is important to him/her, regardless of language ability.
- including a piece of writing from each class so that parents will see their child's class as involved.
- keeping old newsletters available, especially in a school with a high student turn-over. When new parents see the newsletter they can quickly visualize the essence of a positive school climate.

The following model has proven successful due initially to the school principal who believed in its potential as a school catalyst, and mandated it as a school initiative. However, the principal made it easy for ownership of the newsletter to become the creation of teachers, parents, and students.

At a staff meeting, the principal proposed the idea of publishing a newsletter that would benefit both home and school. A committee was formed comprising parents and the principal. (It might be appropriate to also include two older students in the school.)

A parent committee member visited all classrooms and explained that each class could contribute pieces they would like to share with a home/school audience. Typically, file folders were collected every three weeks, giving the committee a week to create the newsletters.

Children were invited to place photocopies of their favorite writings in the file folder. The number of contributions varied from month to month. For those months when only five or six pieces of writing were submitted, class selection was not necessary. When the number of pieces submitted was substantially higher, students assisted in selecting the pieces that best represented the class voice. It was a useful reflection on classroom growth in writing.

Reminders on the P.A. and the teachers' sign-in book helped maintain the school's commitment to collect work samples. Within six months, the school population developed a strong sense of ownership of the newsletter and its place in the school's activities was firmly entrenched.

KEW NEWS
KEW BEACH PUBLIC SCHOOL

"A Story for You. . ."
ROOM 304 (L.D.)
Room 304 started a collective story and the whole third floor helped finish it.

R. 304
Suddenly there it was before me! I couldn't believe my eyes!

R. 303
There was an enormous, scary shark. It was headed right for me.

R. 312
I swam as fast as I could, but the shark was gaining on me. I have never been much of a swimmer, so I gave it a kiss!

R. 311
The shark's eyes bulged and he began to blush. His eyes slowly began to close. He rolled over and I realized that the shark had fainted.

R. 310
I turned around to swim away and there before me was a long line of sharks waiting for a kiss.

R. 309
After I rubbed each of their tummies, I decided that I should

get out of there before anything else happened.

R. 301/2
The news about the sharks and me spread pretty fast, because when I got to shore I found a whole line of animals waiting for a kiss and a belly rub, so I gave them all a kiss and a belly rub.

R. 305
When I got home even the members of my family were lined up for a kiss and a belly rub. Suddenly I woke up and found that all this had been a bad dream; however, outside my room my dog rolled over, anxious for his kiss and belly rub.

R. 308
J'ai mal aux mains et j'ai mal aux levres,

mais mon chien est content!
FIN

Student Comments
"Recommending Books"
Since we have started the readathon, I have read 11 great books. My favourite books were "Way Side Stories" and "Way Side School is Falling Down." If you like books that make you laugh, I recommend these books to you. . . .
Michelle Walker

"Family Language"
The things I liked best about Family Language were the storytellers, Secrets of the Family, the Potatoes and the Pigs. There is nothing I didn't like. I liked bringing my Dad.
Alex Armstrong

Calendars

Weekly Calendars

Many schools publish a weekly calendar outlining upcoming events to help support busy families. Parent (and teacher) knowledge and understanding of weekly events before they occur aids organization. The calendar also presents to parents tangible evidence of the school's strengths, foci, and commitment to education. Due to the frequency of publishing, one administrator or staff member should be responsible for collating the information.

Monthly Calendars

Many schools send out monthly calendars to help families with long-term planning. The administration lists upcoming school-wide events before passing the calendar to the classroom teacher who notes additional classroom information. This advance information, combining parent meetings, school-wide events, and classroom schedules keeps parents well informed. When monthly (or weekly) calendars are sent to the homes, parents have more advance notice of events they would like to attend. This alleviates the stress of sending, and receiving, last-minute invitations.

Yearly Calendars

Although not as flexible as monthly and weekly calendars, yearly calendars can outline for families official school holidays, P.D. days, and special events (e.g., concerts) that will take place during the coming year. This calendar gives a quick overview of the upcoming school year that some families might find helpful, particularly those whose children are new to the school. One school distributes a yearly calendar that contains children's illustrations for each month.

School Surveys

School surveys are multi-faceted and can be used for many purposes. They provide a democratic data bank on the basis of which decisions can be made to stop, start, or change an educational process. The most beneficial school surveys elicit responses from parents, educators, and students.

As an example, surveys can be used to determine what topics parents would like addressed at school community council meetings throughout the year, thereby assisting planning. Such information identifies parent priorities and ensures that the needs of the entire parent community are being addressed. A survey can also identify the times parents prefer to meet with teachers and attend meetings.

Surveys can be used as a strong assessment tool. They can be used to evaluate teacher, parent, and student response to specific school programs. Surveys provide information in measuring the success of parent/teacher interviews and educational programs for parents, as well as to determine the level and types of involvement parents engage in throughout a school year.

Surveys can determine how parents feel about the school. They can identify if the school and staff appear welcoming to parents and students. Parents can comment if newsletters, parents' libraries, and so on create positive feelings about the school within the community.

Meaningful Memory

At Pat's school, a survey was recently distributed in two different forms to both the teaching staff and parents who were either active volunteers, or aspiring to be.

Both the teachers and administrators of the school verified the need for a re-assessment of volunteer uses. Under the guidance of the vice-principal, a small committee of parents and teachers was instigated to study the situation. As a result of this cooperative effort, two different survey sheets were distributed questioning the vision of both the home and school re: the criteria for volunteers. A helpful set of "guiding responsibilities" was established that met the needs of all adults and ultimately, the students of the school.

CHAPTER FOUR

School Matters

Local School Team

"The evidence suggests that no other single focus has the potential to be as productive for students as the close linking of home and school."

Toronto Board Research on Parental Involvement, 1987

Using the Local School Team as a means of monitoring and assisting students with special needs, especially those at-risk, is most beneficial to all concerned — students, teachers, and parents.

What follows are descriptions of two school models, one used in a middle-class area, the other in an inner-city area. Both models incorporate the input and support of parents.

Local School Teams who invite parents to be part of the problem-solving discussion around their children support many messages. One is that parents have a *right* to information about their child's school progress, particularly parents of at-risk students. As well, parents are *responsible* for exploring with the school ways in which their child may need support. Parents might have to adapt and evaluate their behavior toward the child to meet his/her needs. Children are part of a family and do not function in isolation. Both the family and the school "own" the problem. Also, parents can recognize that the school values the partnership of parents.

Model A

The regular team comprises the principal and/or vice-principal, resource room teachers, appropriate classroom teachers, a psychoeducational consultant, and a social worker. Optional team members are the parent(s), support staff (e.g., school nurse), and the student's former teacher. The team meets for a half-day, usually every other week or as school needs determine.

Parents are invited to the team meeting during a second meeting that usually takes place six to eight weeks after the first meeting. They are informed about the reasons students are coming to team and the strategies teachers have employed. Involvement helps parents to understand the steps the school has taken and to be aware of future plans for the student.

The Local School Team is involved in promoting parent understanding and support. If requested by the School Community Council, a workshop on the process is presented yearly to parents. If possible, make a video of the team so that you may show it to parents to give them an idea of its responsibilities. When a child is designated as Learning Disabled, the school offers the family assistance through a Learning Disabled Parents' Support Group.

Model B

At an inner-city school parents are encouraged to be a part of the Local School Team process. Classroom teachers invite parents to come to the first local school team meeting for their child as this is perceived to be more welcoming than a letter or a call from the office. Hopefully, a parent coming into the meeting views the classroom teacher as his/her advocate.

Parents are encouraged to be contributing participants in the meeting. Every effort is made to help parents feel welcome and at ease. If parents attend the meeting, a friendly form letter outlining collaborative goals for both home and school is sent home. If parents are unable to attend, a letter is sent to the home that briefly outlines the nature of the team discussion and any future plans that were finalized. Parents are also informed of approximate dates for the next meeting to discuss outcomes. A contact person at the school offers parents help, answers queries, translates language difficulties, and so on.

Prior to inviting parents to come to the Local School Team, team members and staff should discuss issues that might arise during meetings. Team members should clearly understand their roles during a meeting. They might want to reach a consensus on the criteria for an at-risk child, a gifted child, promotion policies, and so on. Staff and Local School Teams might want to develop a list of the kind of work samples teachers might bring to meetings to develop consistency throughout the school. The holistic scoring method of assessing language might be considered. As well, members consider efforts that help to provide a warm, friendly climate especially for parents, bearing in mind the ratio of teachers to parents is usually 6:1. Such a meeting can be intimidating for parents. Try to set them at ease, keep the meeting on time, and show that you value their time and consideration. If it is appropriate, have the child, teacher, and classroom parent meet after the meeting to discuss their reactions and feelings to issues raised.

An Alternative Model for Local School Teams Using Holistic Scoring

The use of holistic scoring as an evaluation tool in written language can provide the teacher with a no-fuss, no-muss approach to assessment. It can be especially effective for the Local School Team when used in early fall.

Holistic scoring identifies the range of student performance in any class. Writing samples can also be scored by grade levels. Once specific strengths and needs of students' writing are identified, team members can collaborate to discuss appropriate programming and useful strategies. Dialogue can evolve between consultants, special education personnel, classroom teachers, administration, and other professional staff. This can serve as an opportunity for busy educators to talk with one another, defend their beliefs, and learn from the experiences of others.

Steps to Holistic Scoring

- Have the school educators agree on the criteria for holistic scoring before using it in the Team. Teachers can be educated in the simple process through a school workshop.
- The teacher considers each writing sample from the class as a whole piece of writing and separates them into piles — 'one' being the lowest and 'five' being the highest.
- Before the Local School Team meeting, the teacher gathers a 'one' and a 'five' pile to show a range of achievement within his/her class.

- Ask team members to quickly look at the five piles to illicit and verify criteria for each level.
- Collaborate to identify teaching practices and strategies that support each level, as well as any glaring special needs. Special need students at each end of the spectrum can be brought to Team individually at a later date.
- Writing samples for each class can be discussed at the beginning and end of the year to show growth.

This process provides each school administrator with an informal assessment profile of how the school is progressing in written language development. Schools that represent ESL students should encourage them to write in their most fluent language.

Learning Disabilities Parents' Support Group

Parents of children newly assessed with learning disabilities are typically as anxious as their children. Their fears of how other students and parents perceive their children and how their children see themselves are easily apparent. As well, parents are concerned about their child's future education, and how the learning disabilities will affect their lives generally. The formation of a parent support group, led by an executive committee and co-chairpersons, can do much to allay these fears.

Parent support groups can plan a number of special events to foster understanding and knowledge of learning disabilities. These include:

- inviting adults with learning disabilities to share their experiences (e.g., dyslexic adults);
- inviting special education educators from local, senior, and secondary schools to speak about their programs;
- watching new L.D. related videos;
- recommending new books;
- obtaining updated board of education and government policies;
- supporting classroom goals and school programs;
- networking in the "workplace" in order to support young L.D. adults.

Another valuable function of the Support Group is to offer assistance to parents of children who have recently been I.P.R.C.'d and are waiting for school placements.

Wouldn't it be great if . . .

all Boards of Education and educators referred to the letters "L.D." as "Learning Differently"?

Professional Development (P.D.) Days

Even if you whisper the words "Professional Development Day" (in-service days) to any parent (who is not a teacher), you will likely receive raised eyebrows! The inconvenience of having to arrange alternate daycare for the regular school day sends many parents into minor convulsions. This negative parental response can be reversed through proof that staff P.D. days benefit students.

To busy teachers, P.D. days can provide a welcome change of pace and a much-needed opportunity to collaborate with colleagues on school initiatives and programs. Well-organized "days" need strong leadership and effective planning. We suggest that each spring, schools establish a small educator-parent committee to plan P.D. Day topics for the next school year. By including a parent representative (or parents) on the committee, a school might transform opposition into support. A staff survey of in-service interests would provide the committee with a direction. An alternate method is to include a thorough write-up about each Professional Development Day in the school newsletter.

Some topics staffs may identify include:

conducting effective parent/teacher conferences
reporting to parents
school/class team building
classroom assessment and evaluation
needs of special education students
needs of ESL students
effectively integrating parents as partners
school values
cooperative grouping/learning
language through curriculum
homework policy
guiding principles of the school
Family Math

planning seasonal science experiments
stages of reading
reading/language strategies
environmental issues
effective study strategies
identifying bias in materials
multi-level programming
school climate
observation and tracking
integration
spelling
drama
classroom management
anti-racist education

A Framework for a P.D. Day

One of the following stimuli could promote staff development
and discussion:

video/film
guest speaker
staff presenter
story/news article
problem/issue
materials/book display
research
a specific teacher's need
a parent's concern

Individual Free Writing

If the staff members have an opportunity to think or write about
personal experiences and knowledge about the topic before the
stimuli, their interest, ownership, and concentration will be
enhanced.

Group Work with Focus Questions

Depending on the size of the staff, educators can work in one
large group or in a few small ones to discuss one or two focus

questions developing out of the stimuli. Sample questions might be:

- What are the implications of this topic for the school?
- What are we currently doing to support this topic?
- What are the blocks to implementation?
- Can your group generate suggestions to help solve this problem?
- When is the best time to implement this program?
- What resources and funds are required to implement this program?

Prioritive Consensus

Following small group discussions, reports are made to the large group. Suggestions are displayed around the room. The staff highlights suggestions they think they could support. The process can now follow one of two routes — the staff can be left with something to think about or something to implement. If implementation is to have the most impact, it should be shared with families.

Reflection, Evaluation, Independent Application

Immediate evaluation of the in-service can be as simple as the staff reflecting on what made the day worthwhile. The principal's role can involve asking for an evaluation of possible changes and growth resulting from future implementations.

Meaningful Memory

Parents were invited to a P.D. Day discussion focussed on increasing academic success for inner-city students. In groups, parents and staff members looked at how they currently support and encourage student learning in both the home and school environments. Together they planned strategies to be implemented in the future.

Wouldn't it be great if. . .

P.D. Days could really be used as a tool to support staff needs?

School-wide Themes

School-wide themes have the potential to create a unifying experience for educators, parents, and students. For families with more than one sibling, themes offer a context for conversation around the shared focus. If the theme is publicized prior to its commencement, parents can direct questions and have involvement throughout the theme. A newsletter can outline the kinds of appropriate questions parents could ask their children at home to help students reflect and "retell" their learning experiences. For example:

- Ask your child about the talk by the visiting author.
- What did s/he learn that was most interesting?
- Our school has been listening to and reading stories about the sea. Ask your child to retell his/her favorite part. It could be retold verbally or in picture form.
- If you like, send any drawings your child has made about the theme to our school for display.

A newsletter can also seek out a pool of parent talent, resources, or interest around the theme. Interested parents can be invited to speak with students from a variety of grade levels. Students could report what they learned to their own class. Parents can be used as an extra resource person during special theme events, for example: cooking, photography, and storytelling. Families provide a natural, enthusiastic audience to celebrate the culmination of the theme. Including parents in the final experience allows them to see evidence of real learning reflecting a variety of levels and creative finished products. Parents can trigger a reflection process in their conversations at home.

Consider School-wide Themes

School-wide themes involve the same process within each classroom as those chosen by individual teachers — questions, learning objectives, building of knowledge, collaborative learning, problem solving, and so on. The only difference is that each teacher and his/her students decide on their particular areas of interest within the topic. Broad decision-making allows for greater ownership among staff and students.

Suggested School-wide Themes

Water
Historical Celebrations
Heroes and Heroines
The Environment
Poetry
Movies
Genres of Books
Community History
Conflict
Friendship
Multicultural Celebrations
Global Awareness
Change
Seniors

Fantasy
Parental Involvement
Values
Technology
Games and Toys
Media
Theatre/Drama
Forms of Art
Forms of Music
Favorite Authors' Week
Sports
Nursery Rhymes and Fairy
   Tales

Successful School-wide Themes

The environmental theme at a city school invited varied and broad responses from staff and students, acknowledging their strengths and interests. These are some of the activities the school was involved in:

- Junior students participated in an Environmental Festival. The games and demonstrations served to stimulate interest and awareness in environmental issues.
- Three teachers organized resource materials for school-wide use. Materials included pamphlets, nonfiction books, newspaper articles, hands-on materials/objects, storybooks, novels, lists of speakers willing to talk with students, addresses for students to write/phone about environmental concerns, field trips, and student-written materials.
- A speaker from the Toronto Recycling Action Committee explained to the students the city's Blue Box Recycling program.
- Grade four classes visited Ecology House before initiating a school recycling program. The students were responsible for the paper collection and sorting process for the program. Proceeds for their efforts were used for the "Guardian of the Rainforest" project that promotes the conservation of the world's rainforests.

- Grade six students collected pop cans for their contribution to the recycling program.
- Classes monitored acid levels in rainwater in the Backyard Acid Rain (BARK) program. They were twinned with classes in the U.S.A and other southern Ontario schools. The collected data was shared between schools to determine the extent of acid rain in various locations. The grade four/five students represented Canada in a banner exchange with a U.S. class to promote the project.
- A grade four class belonged to the World Wildlife Fund's "Operation Lifeline" program through which they studied endangered species. Proceeds from popcorn and craft sales were donated to the World Wildlife Fund's endangered species research and conservation projects.
- Students took part in "Penny Day" collections and activities that provided both fun and funds for favorite environmental causes.
- A grade five/six class designed vests with the assistance of a visiting artist. These vests and a student written commentary were presented during Education Week to parents and at a fashion show at City Hall. In an interview on a radio station, students shared their concerns and solutions about the environment.
- A week long school-wide drama experience involved students in role playing, creating environments, drawing, making music, and problem solving based on the environmental theme book, *The Two Islands*. Classes rotated throughout the school to hear how different rooms had solved an issue reflected in the story.
- Students wrote environmental messages and presented them on the P.A. to promote environmental awareness during "Environment Week".
- In "Pitch-in Week" activities, the entire school cleaned up the school yard and the adjoining park. The "garbage" was classified as "biodegradable" or "garbage" before being disposed of.
- An environmental group assisted classes in arranging plays and a drama experience where students had to decide where an incinerator was to be built.
- Various artists worked with students to create environmental songs, poetry, and art.

A new principal and his staff developed a school-wide theme

around water. Early in the new year, staff and consultants brainstormed possible directions that the theme could take, potentials for curriculum integration, and available resources. During the next few months, classrooms developed their own foci of interests that evolved out of the theme. The theme culminated during Education Week. The entire school reflected the different interpretations around the theme through art work, student writing, music, drama, mathematics displays, science activities, and so on. Families, courtesy of the school community council, enjoyed a submarine sandwich dinner together. Following dinner, they were encouraged to tour the classrooms. A checklist containing questions about each room's presentations was distributed to each family. At the end of the evening, there was a lucky draw using the questionnaires. The response of the parental community was extremely positive.

At another school, an alternative approach to Young Authors' Week provided a monthly opportunity for school-wide sharing of student writing. Outlined below is the process for Meet the Authors Morning.

Any student with writing to share was invited to the library. One student's writing was profiled each month. The student was asked in advance to prepare a presentation about his/her writing process. S/he explained to students where the stimulus for the story came from, the rationale for choice of words, stages of the revising process, and so on. One student's reflections offered other students an opportunity to hear another writer's thoughts and the way s/he worked through the writing.

In advance, teachers cut six squares of various colored paper. On arrival, students were each given one square of colored paper. Students from the same class were given different colors to create heterogeneous groups, reflecting a variety of age levels. Each student then joined others whose papers were the same color. Students introduced themselves before reading their writing to the others in the group. Students questioned and were questioned about their ideas and thinking processes. In addition, parents could be invited in as part of the audience, during the day or as an evening event, to share writing. Teachers and parents could also bring their writing to share with a group.

Cookies and Young Author ribbons were distributed to each participant at the end of the meeting. This program offered students a vehicle to meet other students in a large, diverse school while sharing writing processes and products.

Wouldn't it be great if. . .

school-wide themes served as a vehicle for teachers to try new learning strategies/models in a collaborative, supportive environment?

School (Af)fairs

"If asked, most parents, teachers and principals will agree that parents need to be involved in and supportive of education. Yet in many places, parents are not actively involved in the life of the school; instead they are spending most of their time and energies organizing bake sales, if they are involved at all"

A. Henderson et al., Beyond the Bake Sale

In this busy decade, when many of us are wearing different hats, we need to take a more candid look at fundraising. The aim is financial gain for schools, but the outgrowth to people involved is fun, team spirit, social interaction, and parents helping other parents. In some school communities, the benefits of fun fairs, bazaars, auctions, and flea markets outweigh the efforts. In others, due to current lifestyles, this kind of fundraising may not be the best use of parents' time.

Schools might consider a number of questions around the issue of fundraising. First, they need to examine the parent community they service and determine if the demands on their parents' time are too great. If the parents lack organizational skill, prepackaged fundraising kits like *Book Fairs* can help create a more successful feeling for all. Also, educators might estimate what percentage of their interaction with parents centers on fundraising. If it is a main focus, schools must decide if this is the best direction for their school/home relations. Finally, is there some vehicle for parent input to teacher and teacher input to parents around fundraising? Some ideas are manageable only with support and understanding from both parties. Everyone involved needs to have feelings of ownership.

Book Fairs

Book Fairs offer educational benefits to families and schools, and support current education programming. They offer another opportunity for parents, educators, and students to interact and make decisions around literature. Students' choice of books offers an observational tool for teachers; children gain something "real" that schools promote. Not only does the child receive a book, but schools win too as classrooms receive books based on total sales. Book Fairs are highly organized and are based on a simple format that doesn't impact negatively on classroom learning time.

Student Recognition

"I now believe there is no biological, geographical, social, economic or psychological determiner of man's condition that he cannot transcend if he is suitably invited or challenged to do so."
Sidney Jouard, Disclosing Man to Himself

Many schools acknowledge students' positive academic and athletic performances. If parents are formally told of their child's special recognition, they are included in the celebration. As teachers, we might forget that positive reinforcement of a child by a school holds great value to a child and their parents. Parents can see this as validating the family's valuing of education. In turn, parents' praise encourages greater student commitment.

Based on the premise that students can choose to be successful, one school chose to recognize students monthly. All school staff were encouraged to nominate students to promote a whole school emphasis. Photos and personal, specific reasons for each student's recognition were placed on a certificate. Letters, translated into a variety of languages, were sent home to parents. Following a display in the library, families received these certificates proudly.

Consider these ways to recognize individuals and groups of students within the school.

- The P.A. is an easy tool to reinforce students. By "catching" students doing something good (e.g., demonstrating positive learning and social behaviors) and announcing it on the P.A., staff, students, and parents on site can take advantage of the knowledge and congratulate students.

- One school keeps a supply of postcards in the office. Each teacher is encouraged to write a postcard to one student weekly, including a positive personal comment. Administrative assistants are responsible for addressing and mailing the cards.
- Some teachers, especially in the inner-city, visit new parents in their homes in an effort to make intimidated parents more comfortable. Visits are kept brief. Teachers might explain a small part of their program, share a toy or a book, or just chat. Teachers offer one positive statement about the family that reflects warmth and caring.

CHAPTER FIVE

Curriculum Matters

Homework (Home Learning)

Home learning provides a natural opportunity for parent, child, and teacher to work cooperatively. It can be a two-way window that reflects how the school supports the child and, in turn, how the parents nourish the child at home. The teacher gets a peek into some of the ways in which the family supports, encourages, and coaches the child. The parents can learn much about the child's self-confidence, learning style, self-control, concentration, independence, and resourcefulness. However, the child, in the middle of these adult resources, will become confused unless both coeducators work together to make expectations clear.

There are four main types of home learning. These may vary from teacher to teacher, grade to grade, and from day to day, as well as in length, content, and difficulty. The four types of learning are:

1. Practice — reinforcing familiar skills
2. Work completion — finishing partly done tasks
3. Preparation or study — reading and reviewing, organizing and memorizing material
4. Extension, creative learning, or enrichment — building on already successful learning, offering processes, ideas, and information in new ways

Listed on the next page are the basic responsibilities of each participant in the home learning triad:

Teachers are expected to:

- try to meet the basic needs, interests, and developmental learning of pupils;
- ensure children's understanding of home assignments;
- vary tasks according to the types of home learning (listed above);
- keep in touch with parents;
- monitor child's work load;
- check assignments frequently;
- be sensitive to the realities of the home climate (e.g., another language spoken in the home, a parent who works at night).

Parents are expected to:

- provide an appropriate environment for each child's learning style;
- ensure that the child has the necessary materials;
- encourage, coach, and show interest;
- avoid judgment statements;
- praise the child's sincere efforts;
- encourage their child to speak with the teacher if s/he is having a problem;
- contact the teacher if home learning is creating stress;
- find out the teacher's expectations.

Children are expected to:

- make sure s/he understands tasks before leaving school;
- take home and return required materials for assignments;
- take responsibility for time management and try to complete tasks on schedule;
- inform parents about their assignments;
- try to work independently, but to ask for assistance if necessary.

Consider these questions:

1. Can recreational reading be considered to be part of home learning?
2. How much time is appropriate to spend on homework tasks?
3. How can a parent provide a good language model if English isn't spoken at home and/or parents are not literate?
4. How might a teacher best communicate with parents regarding home activities, projects, and so on?

5. What is the best way for children to do their tasks at home (eg., radio on or off, alone or with a friend)?
6. How can a parent help with remedial work?
7. In what ways should a teacher be responsible for returned assignments?
8. How can a parent help an older child who no longer wants "interference" from that parent?

Strategies for Reading and Study Assignments

Many children are inclined to read or study material as if they were taking a dose of medicine — swallow it as fast as you can and get it over with. It sounds like a good idea, but it doesn't work. Ask students to consider the following strategies.

A   Use the SMART Strategy

S —et a goal for your task
M—ake a plan
    What materials, resources do I need?
    What do I already know?
    What else do I need to know?
    How will I go about my plan?
A —ttempt the plan
R — eview
    Am I getting close to my goal?
T — hink and reflect

B   Make a "Study Buddy" sheet

- Divide a sheet into two columns, and write "Questions — where? when? who? why? what? how?" at the top of one column, and "Word Box" at the top of the other column. On the 'question' side of the sheet, see how many of these question words you can briefly answer from the reading assignment. On the 'word box' side, write in any clue or important words you meet as you read.
- "Chunk" new material under main headings you are already familiar with. For example, if you already know the provinces of Canada, sort the main cities under each provincial heading.

(Projects: See Project Partners, pg. 85)

Home Reading Programs (Borrow a Book)

"Marie Clay's studies showed very clearly that those children who were "at risk" in learning to read once they entered school, were children who had been deprived of preschool experiences with books in the typical bedtime story situation. These children, it seemed, had not been able to develop a "set towards literacy". They had been unable to build the necessary concepts about print and reading that their more favoured classmates had succeeded in mastering."

David B. Doake, An Overview of Suggestions to be Made for Those Parents Who Want to Help Their Children Learn to Read

Many educators struggle to design appropriate, relevant homework assignments that are easily integrated in to classroom planning. *Borrow a Book*, by Linda Hart-Hewins and Jan Wells (Scholastic, 1988) is a successful reading program delivered in many schools and individual classrooms to support children's reading development. The strength of the program is its ability to deepen positive connections between children, parents, and teachers.

Simply put, a Home Reading program involves students choosing books to read to their parents, read with their parents, or have their parent(s) read to them each night.

Benefits of Home Reading

Good curriculum programming provides a number of educational outcomes for a variety of audiences. A home reading program supports parents, children, and teachers.

Home Reading programs are a boon to busy parents who are often unable to access appropriate reading materials for their children. These helpful programs also provide a window into student learning in all the language strands. Many parents have been better able to discover their children's interests, personal tastes, and feelings through such programs. They assist parents in understanding the methods for teaching reading in today's schools, and in developing trust in the reading process. These classroom initiatives help parents recognize their critical roles in developing the literacy of their children. They also provide, in families with more than one child, an opportunity to recognize individual abilities, reading developmental levels, and learning strengths of each child.

For the student, a reading program establishes a consistent reading ritual at home, sometimes even introducing the practice in homes. It allows the child to hear another fluent reader who can lend support and encouragement to him/her. We have all heard the adage, "Practice makes perfect". Nothing we can think of supports this statement more than its application to reading. In a home reading program, an early reader is offered the opportunity to read individually and regularly with a positive adult. Reading that is practised within a caring climate builds self-esteem. Being responsible for carrying books to and from home helps children to develop independence and pride in completing a task successfully.

Schools and teachers also gain by introducing the program. The program introduces reading into some homes, thereby promoting equity of opportunity. It is easy to set up and administer, in both the classroom and the home. Home Reading programs can also form the basis for appropriate homework policies in the primary grades and answer parents' homework queries. The program sends a powerful message to parents regarding their importance in developing their children's literacy and emphasizes a shared responsibility for learning.

A reading program shared by a loving parent is one of the few effective levers we have that compete with television and computer games. These programs strengthen positive social interaction between parent and child, and become a potential springboard for shared discussion. They are powerful tools that help to bridge the child's two most important learning contexts, and provide families with another opportunity to celebrate small but valuable successes. They offer everyone involved a definite role, thereby empowering students, parents, and teachers alike.

What a Home Reading Program Looks Like in the Classroom

Within the classroom, Home Reading offers an established daily time for children to return and choose books. Children are able to pull a book from a selection that coincides with their individual reading ability, as books are grouped by levels of difficulty. Each child is guided to the group of books that support his/her stage of reading development. S/he can record the date and name of the book they have decided to take home. A child may choose to take the same book for a number of evenings. This should be allowed as it is a student's choice, and offers him/her a risk-free opportunity to read. The student and teacher can use these books as vehicles for discussion around personal choices, books genres, and general responses to reading. A weekly book club may develop within the classroom. This allows for shared interaction between a reader and an audience. It's also exciting to observe an older reader who has practised a book at home choose to reread the story to a younger reading buddy. Teachers, in turn, learn more about each student's comprehension of text, organizational skills, and personal interest. Students learn more about themselves, build on their experiences, and are part of a classroom committed to reading. They are better able to integrate the elements found in good literature into their own personal writing. Students will soon see themselves as readers and writers, and will carry their reading bags home with satisfaction.

What a Home Reading Program Looks Like

A parent and student will be asked to set aside ten to fifteen minutes each evening as reading time. One of these reading situations will occur: parent reading to child, child reading to a parent, or parents and child reading in a shared experience.

Parents will need to understand the ambiance around reading a story and hearing their child read aloud. They may need to be trained to respond positively to student attempts, offer suggestions to support approximations, and read aloud with fluency and expression to engage students in the books. Parent and child should seek out a comfortable setting without distraction. Establish a reading ritual at bedtime or a special shared quiet time (e.g., after dinner). These are 'best practices' in many literate homes. We support the idea that teachers send a journal home in each book bag. When a book is finished, both parents and child can briefly comment on the literature before returning the response journal to the school.

We suggest that the book bag home and school habit occur each school day. With this powerful daily home support, children recognize the value that their significant adults place on reading.

Consider:

• making a Home Reading program in all the primary grades so parents do not see one primary program as "better" than another;

- delegating work to a number of teachers to lessen the load for all.

Decide on these basic questions.

1. *Where might you apply for funding to acquire books?*

   Some boards have specific funding available through curriculum departments. Consider holding book fairs, approaching the School Community Council for funds, or drawing up a proposal for the superintendent.

2. *Does the principal have a role to play in the implementation?*

3. *What kind of literature will you buy for each level of reading development?*

   Borrow a Book provides suggestions that will help you make your buying decisions. With fellow educators, collaboratively sort books into different levels.

4. *What kind of bags will you use?*

   Some staffs use ziplock freezer bags as they are inexpensive and reasonably sturdy. Label the bags with the students' names. Other schools invest in or sew sturdy canvas bags.

5. *How will parents become aware of the program and their role in it?*

   Some staff introduce the program at a "Meet the Teacher Night," held early in the fall, while others hold a special meeting to share information with parents. One staff created a video for parents that modelled positive interaction between a "parent" and a child. Parents could view the video at home or at the school.

6. *How might this program be used in schools where parents are illiterate or are unable to read in English?*

   Taped books and stories offer an excellent opportunity for whole families to hear stories together. Parents and children can use taped books as a vehicle for strengthening literacy within a home. Some schools collect bilingual or unilingual books written in languages other than English to encourage parents to read in their own language. Research has shown that when students are literate in one language, the acquisition of a second language is much easier. Translations of information will need to be available when necessary.

7. *What system might teachers use to track books?*

Some teachers use library pockets labelled with each child's name. Students place cards with book names into their pocket each day. Other teachers ask students to record the book they are borrowing on a sign-out sheet or book.

8. *How will you evaluate the program?*

Review parent and student comments concerning the program. The opinions provided in the journals are valuable as they reflect the attitude of those most affected by the program. Observe students' growth as readers.

9. *Where does it fit in the school day?*

Teachers prefer setting aside time for the program at the beginning or the end of the day. It typically takes about fifteen minutes.

10. *Can this program be adapted for the junior grades?*

Staffs might discuss creating a Home Reading program for older students. Chapter books might not be returned daily, but a reading log and comment card or response journal would be useful. Books read at home could be discussed in small groups afterward to provide students with book suggestions and to foster discussion.

Meaningful Memory

A parent at Queen Victoria shared that the Home Reading program had been instrumental in building her relationship with her younger son. She commented on the closeness of their relationship and of her understanding of his reading development. She welcomed the daily ritual of sharing a book and felt more supportive of him in all of his school endeavors. The positive sharing of stories that had been modelled for her provided direction in dealing with her son in other social/academic areas. Her older son had not been part of the program and she was aware of the difference in their relationship.

each class involved in the program developed an attitude toward reading similar to that witnessed in an adult book club?

situations developed where children used literature to explore and develop their own personal growth and an understanding of their worlds.

Share-a-Tape Program

Share-a-Tape is a new idea that came to mind as a result of a recent classroom activity. While studying a unit on our country, we invited parents and/or grandparents, through our newsletters, to share their experiences. Robin's grandparents, both age seventy-eight, live in a small town outside of the city and were unable to respond in person. They had both experienced interesting childhoods and were keen to share their memories with the children in our class. Robin, with tape recorder in hand, visited his grandparents. With their assistance, he formulated a set of ten questions he wanted to pose to these venerable citizens and became an interviewer. Robin, who is a quiet boy in class, blossomed in his role and used strong interviewing skills. His grandparents responded superbly and shared childhood memories that fascinated the students in our class.

The program has great potential for strengthening effective language skills. At present, the program is being expanded into a school initiative. Each class who wishes to take part in the Share-a-Tape program can build their own class library at their listening center or add to a school tape library of theme experiences.

We live in an era where we seem to experience sound only when it is accompanied by a video picture or when it is blasted at such an incredible level that it threatens our hearing and pollutes neighborhoods. It is time to encourage better listening strategies within our classrooms.

Family Math / Family Science

These programs offer families opportunities to problem solve, risk-take, explore, question, build, and collaborate while focussing on science and mathematics curriculum areas. Activities are workshop-based, involving parents, educators, and children. *Family Math*, by Jean Kerr Stermork et al. (University of California) details complete plans that can help you create a series of evenings for your parent community. Because of the success of the book, a book on family science is in development.

A program based on *Family Math* has been offered for four years at one school. Over a series of evenings, parents began to relate more positively to their children, provide thoughtful questions, and encourage their children to think about their answers. Also noticed during this time was a change in some parents' voice tones, body language, and level of warmth exuded when interacting with their children.

The "Family Math" committee identified student needs within the school, and collected math activities to support these needs that families could work on. The intent was to help parents become aware of how they might help at home and to increase their understanding of specific student needs.

The "Family Science" program was developed and delivered with the aid of two parents working in the school. The "Family Math" committee utilized parents to organize the evenings. It was felt that parent support in delivery offered other parents a meaningful opportunity to support children's education, provide a strong model for other parents taking part in the tasks, and give an opportunity for parents to shape the development of parent in-service.

If you plan a parent/child evening to work on activities consider:

- using your understanding of student needs to shape the experiences and activities offered;
- arranging translators if required. Families of one language group tend to sit together so people can translate within the group. Remember that children can serve as interpreters. Another option is to invite English-speaking families and one other dominant language group to work together;
- supplying a babysitter for very young children;
- asking each member of the committee to be responsible for one specific activity (e.g., supplying materials, directions);
- having committee parents give instructions and explain activities to other parents;

- inviting the children to design and send out the invitations;
- offering refreshments for both adults and children during the evening;
- placing the materials for each activity in tubs for a quick set up and clean up;
- presenting activities in an educational context so parents can identify the learning involved;
- offering small prizes for various reasons;
- taking photos for a bulletin board or newsletter, or videotaping the event to enjoy later;
- creating an evaluation for both parents and children to fill out collaboratively;
- making the evening relatively short so children aren't too tired the next day;
- inviting students to reflect on the evening the next day and share the experience.

Science Fairs

The established model of science fairs present some difficulties in both the school and the home. Families with access to materials, talent, and related experiences often produce high-quality products that reflect the parent as much as the child. Other children are without extra assistance to help create the same polished product, thereby creating inequity and some frustration.

Two models that have been used to address this equity issue are as follows.

1. Science Fairs are recognized by the school as a collaborative family project. Families are encouraged to work together at home to prepare for a school display/presentation.

2. Children are invited to work on the project during school hours, and exclude parental involvement. Children use the resources and materials available in the classroom. They may do the project in pairs, and use one another as resources.

In reflecting on the value of these models, we devised a third model to consider called Project Partners. This model is elaborated on the next page.

Project Partners

Language, in its varied forms, links with all curriculum areas. It is the constant presence in all subject areas that helps children construct meaning and understanding. Through the use of projects, families can explore and share their learning and experiences on any question or area of interest.

We have developed Project Partners as a model that provides equity of opportunity to all students in project work, especially work previously completed at home. Students, depending on the support and resources available at home, create projects with varied levels of parental support ranging from strong parent commitment to total abstinence. However, the level of parent guidance and support offered can affect the process and product students are engaged in. Project Partners legitimizes the idea that the family gains recognition as a cooperative, active unit with the project process.

The benefits of this model are many. Educators are able to offer on-the-spot assistance, encouragement, and resources available to all participants. In using resource texts, students can be guided and supported by both parent and teacher. Paper and creative tools can be supplied by the school, an assurance that all families have access to materials. Families can learn from one another in planning, developing, and enhancing research skills, as well as presenting finished products.

A joint criteria about the projects can be developed before the projects begin, using child, parent, and teacher input. This develops a shared understanding of the task and commitment involved and the nature of the projects. Planned evenings allow that the time commitment remains the same for all families. The project completion time frame mirrors the number of evenings families attend. Educators, in a leadership role, have the opportunity to present literature to enrich the project focus. Families will benefit from the social climate developed among the participants, creating another "community of learners". Parents with limited language and/or ideas can be identified and given additional support by school staff. Students can see a successful partnership between home and school: the process will support the product.

Format

Use a broad topic in one of the curriculum areas. Possible topics are:

social studies (history) — environment, law, government,
science — inventors,
mathematics — technology,
music — instrument, famous musicians,
art — famous artists, styles of art, architecture
drama — storytelling, role playing, resolving a conflict
language — publishing a book, creating a diorama in response
   to a story
physical education — develop a game

Hold a series of evenings for individual families to work on projects together at school. Each family will choose a project topic related to the unit decided on through the group's initial planning.

The first evening . . .

1. Model for parents the steps in doing a project, for example, identify an area of interest within the broader topic, brainstorm possibilities, identify questions, explore and skim varied resources, retrieve and organize information, decide on how to present it, and identify relationship to our world.

2. Develop and present criteria for the project (both process and product).

3. Offer families time and space to work through the process. Educators are available as a resource when needed.

4. Read appropriate literature for families at the evening's end. This provides a shared experience and winding-down period.

5. Find a place to store projects until the next evening.

On the following evenings . . .

- Begin with selected literature.
- Offer time and support families to continue their work.
- On the final evening, plan for presentations that reflect the choice and comfort level of the participants.
- Give families an opportunity to evaluate and reflect on the process and their learning.

CHAPTER SIX

Language Partners

An Introduction to Language Partners

Language Partners first evolved from an enjoyable classroom activity that Pat and her students embarked upon one day. The class had brainstormed a collective list of autumn words they wanted to work with. They paired up to write simple autumn poems using the same word list. The students were so pleased with the results that they asked to take the poems home. On the following Monday, Thomas arrived at school glowing over a poem about fall that he and his mother, step-father, and uncle had written at home. It was fantastic and the others were green with envy over Thomas's successful venture. Not to be outdone, the other students hurried home to perform the same task.

Given Thomas's experience, Pat began to think about the idea of developing a family-type language program for others. If it worked for her reluctant writers, it could prove to be an enjoyable challenge for other families. Pat's principal supported her idea and a program was born.

The "baby" has not been without its burps, and even some minor belches. However, on the whole, Language Partners has been a huge success. Her new Learning Disabled group, some of whom took part in the initial program, continue to ask for more as do their parents. The school's Parent/Teacher organization has asked the program be done again — a testimony to its success.

Thanks go to Maureen and Pat's team-teaching colleague Noreen Houghton, for making the program a truly cooperative, problem-solving adventure.

Strengths of Language Partners

- It is an adaptable program that draws in community, school, and parent talents to support learning.
- The evening focus can be extended into classroom themes and learning.
- It mirrors classroom practice.
- Language Partners illustrates how enjoyment and engagement stimulate learning.
- The program demonstrates how learning takes place within a strong social context.
- The generic model is limited only by educators imaginations and school needs.
- It is a teacher-driven model that encourages teacher planning and collaboration.
- Language Partners encourages student involvement in planning, organizing the evening, and presenting it to parents.
- The program can be shaped to work with specific parents around educational needs of students, for example, at-risk readers.
- Language Partners is built on the premise that in order for parents to understand current education, they need to experience it.
- It is inexpensive and relatively easy to organize.

Language Partners

We thought about the concept of education and its relationship to children and the community in past decades before considering how these relationships have evolved over time to their current state. Programs like Language Partners support today's children, parents, and communities.

CHILD'S PERCEPTION

FAMILIES IN PREVIOUS GENERATIONS	SCHOOLS IN PREVIOUS GENERATIONS
defined roles	defined roles
structure	structure
adult control, decision making	adult control, decision making
stabilized families	stabilized schools
reading, oral storytelling = entertainment	reading = academic success
trust in schools	trust in home
expectation of pre-determined paths, accepted failure	expectation of predetermined paths, accepted failure
extended family, community support	community support

CHILD'S PERCEPTION

FAMILIES OF TODAY

confusion about family members'
   roles, methodology, educational
   goals
tolerance, promotion of individual
   differences
greater options for parent roles
greater responsibility for family unit
less reading than television

SCHOOLS OF TODAY

confusion about values, varied child-
   rearing methods
greater options for teaching and
   learning styles
greater responsibility for teaching
   whole child (holistic approach)
   individual differences

PARENT'S PERCEPTIONS OF SCHOOLS TODAY

empower parents to recognize their
   importance as educators
opportunities to see child's learning
   group situations
more open communication with
   educators
greater understanding and trust of
   educators
family outreach
vehicle to practise good teaching/
   learning practices
opportunity for growth and collaboration between families

TEACHER'S PERCEPTIONS OF SCHOOLS TODAY

empower educators to recognize
   parents as educators
opportunity to see parent/child interaction
more open communication with
   parents
community outreach
vehicle to model good teaching/
   learning practices
opportunity for growth and collaboration between educators

CHILD'S BELIEFS

common belief and actions systems
cooperative positive support system
opportunities for discussions about learning
social liaison between educators and parents

Format

Each session builds in a sequence of components necessary for a strong learning experience. This format presents a good teaching framework for parents to understand.

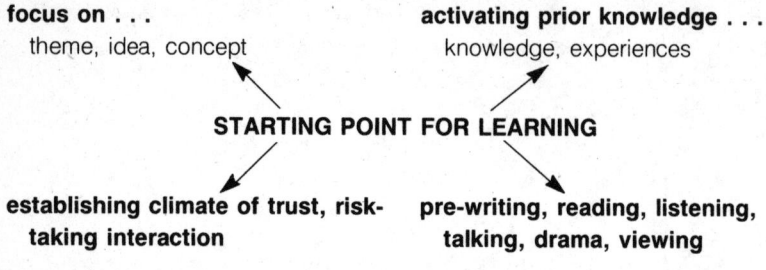

focus on . . .
   theme, idea, concept

activating prior knowledge . . .
   knowledge, experiences

STARTING POINT FOR LEARNING

establishing climate of trust, risk-taking interaction

pre-writing, reading, listening, talking, drama, viewing

```
LOOKS LIKE

Stream of consciousness writing
Sematic mapping
Sharing of experiences
Exploration
```

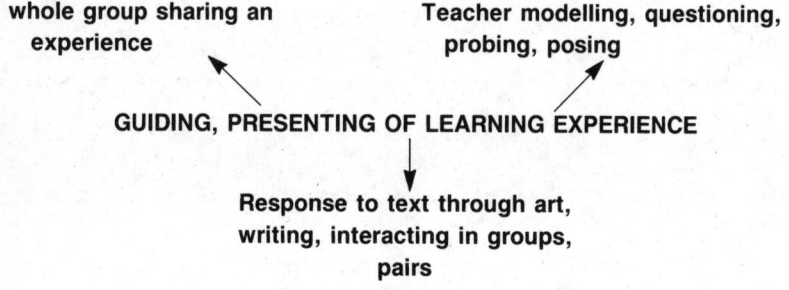

whole group sharing an experience

Teacher modelling, questioning, probing, posing

GUIDING, PRESENTING OF LEARNING EXPERIENCE

Response to text through art, writing, interacting in groups, pairs

```
LOOKS LIKE

Reading a story or a poem
Showing a video
Presenting a guest speaker
```

applying critical thinking skills,
developing and responding to
questions

personalizing the experience

ENRICHING AND PRACTISING

parent and child collaboration

extending ideas

```
+-----------------------------------------------+
|                  LOOKS LIKE                   |
|                                               |
|   Families discussing their understanding     |
|           of the text, relating it to         |
|             personal experiences              |
+-----------------------------------------------+
```

empowering parents to facilitate
their children's learning

learners applying framework to
other situations

CLASSROOM/HOME APPLICATION EXTENSION

```
+-----------------------------------------------+
|                  LOOKS LIKE                   |
|                                               |
| Parents and children interacting positively,  |
|         incidentally about learning           |
|      Families using learning strategies        |
|       Homework, Handouts for Parents           |
|               Parent questions                |
|     Classroom teachers extending theme,        |
|             independent learning              |
+-----------------------------------------------+
```

Language Partners Model

Objectives

To involve students, parents, and teachers together in language activities that promote learning. The evenings should be: fun, relaxing, informative, noncompetitive, nonthreatening, and informal

Number

The program can be held once a week for a month, once a month, or at the beginning or culmination of a theme.

Approximate Length

The evening program should be approximately 1.5 hours. Should participants wish to continue, you can use another half-hour without tiring most parents and children.

Who

Each meeting should comprise the teacher (or teachers) of the class (classes) involved, other planners (if any), and support staff appropriate for that evening (e.g., the principal, the school librarian, the vice-principal, guest readers). If the children in the classroom are actively involved in the planning, setting up, and delivering of the program, a strong learning opportunity is utilized. The classroom teacher is the key player.

Where

Use pleasant spaces that accommodate up to forty people. In our school, the library was the main meeting area and families spilled out into the adjacent staffroom and into our hall. For practical reasons, our limit for the Language Partners evenings was twenty families per evening. The same families came for all four evenings.

Pre-planning

Since Pat was the original instigator of the program, she wished to involve her ten Learning Disabled students (reluctant readers) and their parents. It was important that they be involved with another group of students approximately their own age. We selected the grade three/four family grouping with which the class integrates. The other grade three/four classes in the school received such great reports about our evenings that they asked to take ownership of four evenings later in the year, and did so.

Planning — Who

One or two combined groups and their parents along with the children's teachers took part in each evening. We feel strongly that our program works best with smaller numbers and with each student's significant adults (parents and the classroom teacher) present. The model is not intended to be effective with large groups (e.g., 40 or more adults).

How

Noreen, the grade three/four teacher, Maureen, and Pat met to set out the criteria and method of inviting families. We designed an invitation that met our needs. Later, an alternative to this system evolved. Students made their own invitations. One word of caution — make sure the personal invitations contain the correct and necessary information. If they don't, the parents will be like the dinner guests who show up on the wrong night! Students might check one another's invitations to see that information is correct. If you list the information to be included in point form on the board, you might allow students to present it in their own way. This could be a valid learning/writing situation.

We designed different themes, with good literature to support the focus. The activities involved all aspects of the language program — listening, speaking, reading, writing, drama, and viewing. The evenings were developed to capitalize on the strengths of school staff, the school storytelling group, guests, and parents whenever possible.

Note:
If the teacher plans a set of evenings for a second year, s/he may find it helpful to include one or two parent volunteers as part of the planning committee. The more creative ideas that are generated, the better the situation. The teacher will need to keep the evenings' themes focused on good literature.

A Typical Evening's Framework (adapt it to your group's needs):

- Introductory activities in the hall (made on large sheets of colorful paper)
  These openers were made to create a comfort level for parents and children as they arrived. We felt it was necessary to have hall activities so that families were involved immediately. This also allows for varying times of arrival, and creates a friendly, social setting. Name tags were worn by those who so wished.
- Informal Welcome
  Staff and guest readers were introduced. The printed menu for the evening was noted, and the theme stated. Participants were made aware of the refreshment corner which was set up for the entire evening. Babysitting arrangements for parents of very young children were explained. Finally, parents were invited to jot down questions about learning and classroom programs during the evening.
- Icebreaker activity for social interaction and to stimulate thinking around the theme
- Story, poetry
- Activity to deepen the text in pairs (parent and child) or small groups (usually four)
- Sharing/second activity
- Reflection, responding to parents' questions, rationale explained for specific learning activities
- Storyteller (student from the school's storytelling group) or parent reader
- Handouts and homework (an activity to be shared by the family during the week)

This format can be used as a Language Partners menu, listing the specific theme and related activities.

The material that follows represents our beliefs about learning as related to the Language Partners program. These statements were shared with the families on the first evening. At the end of the four evenings, the parents were asked to assess their experiences in relation to these beliefs.

Guiding Principles of Language Partners

Learning develops:

- when families identify and build on children's interests;
- when families focus on children's strengths;
- through positive interaction and investigation of shared experiences;
- when families are actively engaged in the thinking process;
- through ongoing support of their children's goals;
- when families value both the processes and products of learning;
- when parents recognize their importance as teachers;
- when home and school invite children to take ownership of reading/language for personal growth;
- when families continue to model a love of language and reading;
- when parents' daily efforts result in long-term growth for their children.

The outcomes of Language Partners should include a sense of success and satisfaction for all participants.

Outcomes

For Parents . . .

- better understanding of educators' objectives;
- deeper understanding of the learning process;
- development of educationally sound interactive strategies (e.g., effective questioning, storytelling, encouraging creative writing, conferencing with their children);
- greater awareness of their child's thinking process and behaviors within a group.

For Children . . .

- an opportunity for social interaction with community members;
- an occasion to experience positive modelling through observing parents, educators, and peers working together in a pleasant climate;
- an understanding that learning can be both fun and engaging.

For Teachers.. . .

- a stronger link with parents;
- a forum for the teacher to see the child functioning within their own family;
- a chance to market good educational practices to parents;
- an opportunity to help impact the way parents relate to children around learning.

Theme Suggestions

We have created other successful Language Partner evenings and are in the process of developing additional plans. With a little imagination, enthusiasm, and planning the program can be adapted to almost any grade level (and school climate) from levels one to eight. *Its beauty lies in its adaptability to your school's unique strengths and needs.*

Some themes you might like to consider are:

color	faces and feelings
grandparents	our senses
school helpers	the seasons (choose one at a time)
shoes	
fairy tales	a book "walk and talk"
legends	trees
cookies	favorite people
pizza	potatoes
heroes	hats
hobbies	dreams
the environment	manners
spaghetti	courage
pigs	relationships
pets	change
windows	sports

Sample Evening Themes

Evening One — *Venn Diagrams*

Openers

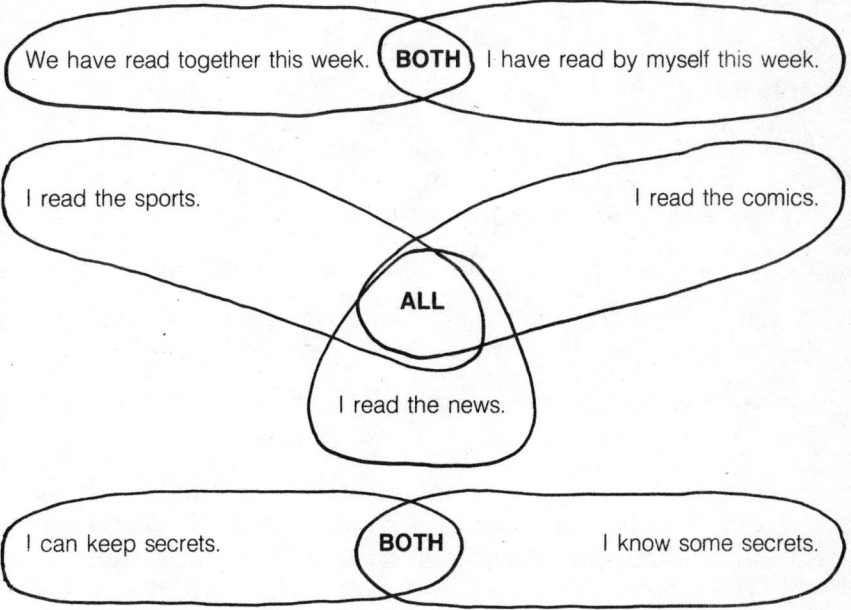

We have read together this week. **BOTH** I have read by myself this week.

I read the sports. I read the comics.

ALL

I read the news.

I can keep secrets. **BOTH** I know some secrets.

or

List all the things we read in our community (e.g., street signs, newspapers, posters, menus, t-shirts, store signs).

Icebreaker

Prior to the evening, children list individually on papers the names of objects that people treasure, and place them in separate envelopes (e.g., family, pets, photographs, family outings).

Each family team is then given an envelope, and these envelopes are exchanged with another team. Both teams open and read envelopes without revealing the items. The teams have to ask questions to guess the name. Questions must be answered with "Yes" or "No". To support families who are unable to guess (after a few minutes) reveal the list of all the names included in the envelopes. This helps everyone feel successful. It is surprising how difficult this activity can be for some, however it is a great warm-up and builds a good climate.

Read *Five Secrets in a Box* by Catherine Brighton (Fitzhenry and Whiteside, 1987), or another book written around the theme of family values.

Activity

Each family is given a paper and two pencils. They are to discuss the five things that are the most important to them. The parents and child create the list together.

1. The families prioritize the objects by importance.

2. Join with another family and share. Volunteers may read their list.

3. Read "Wilfred Gordon McDonald Partridge", or another story about a relationship between two or more people.

4. Distribute bags containing an assortment of family memorabilia. Two families form a group to discuss the contents of the bag. Students may be involved prior to the evening by deciding what might constitute people's treasures. They could collect items from home to include in the bag (e.g., sheet music, a jewelry box, sports badges, photographs, a watch, a necklace, a lace collar, a book, a letter, etc.).

5. Families look at the memorabilia and think about:
   "Who was in this family?"
   "What do these treasures tell about them?"
   "What can you guess or imagine things about them?"
   Choose two people you feel were in the family. Talk about their relationship, using the items found in the bag.

6. Families might list:
   "What we know about this family"
   "What do we not know about this family"
   "What might be true"
   Choose one person in the family. Create a description of this

person — what s/he likes, doesn't like, where s/he lives, his/her age, and so on. Talk to your group about this person.

Questions, Homework

Students may wish to write out the description of their character and bring it to the next Language Partners to share.

Families might ask other members at home what their list of five important things would be, and record their list. (Author's note: Thanks to Ron Benson for the use of this idea in relation to *Five Secrets in a Box*).

These activities offer parents and children the opportunity to collaborate, reach consensus, and imagine. Students and their families can develop clearer ideas when they listen to the ideas of others and handle real materials. Parents are also given a window into the values of their child, and vice versa.

Evening Two — *Games*

Opener

Families are given a piece of equipment, for example, a ball, a hoop, a bean bag, or a die. They are instructed to design a game using the piece of equipment. They must decide the number of players, the object of the game, and its rules. After devising and playing their game briefly, families meet with another family and teach them the game. Here are some of the games/activities you might wish to try.

Twenty Questions

This game is similar to the traditional twenty questions, but it incorporates listening, speaking, writing, reading, knowledge, and critical thinking skills. Model the game first. Think of a literature genre (e.g., mystery, science fiction, sports). The person or thing you are thinking of must be a part of a book. Parents and children get twenty guesses to identify the object or person.

Divide a piece of paper in two columns, one labelled "Yes", the other "No". To answer each of the questions, write the answer in the proper column. If a child asks, "Is s/he funny?"

and the answer is a detective, then you would write, "S/he is funny". As the families ask their twenty questions, a list of criteria about the object/person appears. Children must read the information before making a guess. This works to eliminate random guessing and promotes critical thinking. Demonstrate the game a few times, then let parents and children try it. Allow both parties to have a few turns.

This game is suitable for car trips, etc. Remind parents that children write the list of criteria. Spelling is not important during the game, but reasonable approximations are encouraged.

Password

This is an excellent game to promote vocabulary development, understanding of concepts, and retrieval of specific language. Prior to the evening and in class, children are asked to work in groups. In these groups, they generate a list of words about a particular subject. They can be descriptive words, action words, or names of people, places, or things. Proper names are not to be used. Categories might include:

- household objects
- feelings, moods
- city and country places
- occupations
- hobbies
- sports
- objects or people related to transportation

The teacher takes the lists and chooses twenty or thirty words, writing each on one piece of paper. Each paper is xeroxed and cut up into sections, one section per word.

At Language Partners, two families sit together. Either children or parents draw a word. They might give one word that reminds them of the word (e.g., the word is 'playground', the first clue might be 'swing"). Each pair gets to hear the clues; clues and guesses alternate between families. Each word can receive ten guesses and clues. The number of points each team receives depends on how fast they guess the word, starting with ten points, and moving to one point. Rhyming words, opposites, and expressions that contain the word can be given.

Explain to parents that relevance and enjoyment are important components that foster learning. If children enjoy an experience, they are more likely to willingly practise it. Both commercial and homemade games can have the potential to promote learning. Parents should think about what skills games might encourage when they purchase/play them.

Skills games promote critical thinking, strategizing (e.g., chess) language development (e.g., Twenty Questions, Password), decision making, planning, (e.g., Risk, Monopoly), deductive reasoning (e.g., Clue), and problem solving (e.g., Chess). Computer games can also promote these same skills (e.g., Where in the World is Carmen Sandiego?). Other games (e.g., Bingo) involve luck and chance, however the social interaction is fun, and time spent together is extremely valuable.

Teaching children games also offers them ways to relate positively and spend time with their friends. Stress the fun aspect and play down the competitiveness. That said, children should have opportunities to play both competitive and cooperative games. Competitive games, if played with a positive spirit where children do not see losing as critical, are valuable. Opportunities to play competitive games in a supportive, fun environment help students accept a loss with some grace and good humor.

Parents also need to consider that the kind of model they present when playing a game will be emulated by their children. Give your best effort; cheating or being ungracious to winners is inappropriate.

Evening Three — Sports

(This was one of two sports evenings we designed. Everyone really enjoyed this theme)

Openers

1. Add to a chart words that describe good sportsmanship, for example, being fair, taking turns, and cooperating.

2. Which sport do you know the most about? Share at least two things you know about it with your parent/child.

3. Write down a statement that you would hear during a sports event, for example, "Did you see that tackle?" Let your parent/child read it and guess the sport.

Icebreaker

Prior to the evening, students list different items of sports equipment on paper. In each envelope, place ten pieces of paper on which are recorded a piece of sports equipment. Families look at the papers, discuss them, and order the papers according to the following categories:

- items that cost the most,
- items arranged from the least expensive to the most expensive,
- items arranged from smallest to largest,
- items arranged from strongest to weakest.

Look at your items. Find as many ways of sorting them as you can, for example, by material and season of use. As families think of another category, they could sort the articles into it.

Story

We invited the school's chief custodian to read a baseball story as he coaches the coed baseball team. He really enjoyed this, as did his audience.

Activities

The parent becomes an interviewer on a TV sports talk show. S/he interviews the child athlete of the year (their child). The child is asked to discuss all the things that make him/her so successful, and to give advice to other athletes.

We used cardboard microphones for this activity. Props can be made by students prior to the evening. Though very simple, the microphones offer parent and child something with which to dramatize. This was a popular activity. The microphone has been used in many classroom activities since its introduction at the Language Partners evening.

Groups of six (three adults and their children) select a sport and then make up a chant of four lines or more that employs vocabulary related to this sport. Ask the group to also make up actions that are related to the sport. They can spend a few minutes trying to capture the sport in various movements. The group takes a rest from physical activity and designs a pennant that gives the team name. The groups present their work — chant, poses, pennant — to other groups. One idea for introducing the presentation is to plan a tableau (people freeze in mid-movement): in this instance, they would freeze in positions that signify the sport.

We invited a high-jumper who trains athletes to discuss his career. He brought a photo album with newspaper clippings to tell his personal story. The students were very interested in this real sports figure.

Questions, Homework

The chanting activity offers parents an opportunity to see how their children work in a group situation, as well as allowing them to be creative together. The interview activity, meanwhile, allows children to create a story using some of their own experiences.

Alternate Activities

Students can look in the sports section of the newspaper for an article on a sports hero. After they have read the article, they can write the information in their own words or list five pieces of information they learned about the athlete.

Students might choose a past or present sports hero, and generate five questions about this person. They can use class, library, and other resources to answer their questions. Students can present their findings in interesting ways to the other students. Research can also be done in pairs.

This theme was so popular that it spilled over into classroom activities and served as the basis for another Language Partners sports evening.

Evening Four — The Writing Process

Opener

Parents and children collaborate to create a list of topics on which they are knowledgeable. Parents are encouraged to draw on their knowledge of their child, for example, hobbies, interests, family trips, and so on. Topics generated can be set aside as the starting points for later writing exercises.

or

If students use the writing process and writing folders, ask them to explain to parents what the process is, show dated writing samples, the format of the writing folder, and so on. Students may plan this explanation in advance, listing the main points to share, practising with a partner, and so on. This provides a real opportunity for children to plan, summarize, and present information. We discovered that the parents really enjoyed hearing about what the children did in class.

or

Model planning a story map. Parents and children choose a favorite story to retell in story map form. This strategy is a useful one for parents and students. Story maps provide a flexible structure incorporating students ideas and offer a sound planning reference.

In this particular Language Partners evening, we simulated the same kind of writing experience students have in school. Students' writing experiences usually take place two or three times a week at specific times in the day. Students also write daily as a method of recording their learning and thinking. Their recording of information, ideas, and so on provides an alternative to workbooks and stencils, where adult writers are responsible for doing the thinking and students have a less important role.

Pre-Writing

Teachers ask parents/children to create an individual list of all their family members. This list may include extended family members who are important to the children. Parents and children are then asked to star the people on the list about whom they could tell a story. The story may be about an event, experience, or a conflict resolution situation.

With the family list in hand, adults and children walk about the room, find a partner, and tell one of the stories. Children talk to adults, adults talk to children. This activity encourages a trusting climate for story writing. Finally, parents find their own children and the parent and child tell a finished version of one of their stories. Each adult and child then chooses one of his/her stories to develop. Depending on the capabilities of the adults and children, stories may be developed collaboratively about a shared experience.

Families individually list all the people involved in the story. They write key words or phrases to describe their appearance, involvement in the story, point of view, characters, and so on. This list is shared between parent and child. It is very important that the parent/child retain ownership of their ideas. Questions may develop, but each person controls his/her own version of the story.

Create a second list. Elaborate on the setting of the story. Where did it happen? Describe the setting, time of day, year, images about the setting, and so on. Think about your feelings around the story, your mood, point of view, problems/resolutions. Briefly write these on a third list. This list is shared between parent and child. Parents and children may talk about their stories, adding details and answering questions about story content.

First Draft

Writers use five to ten minutes to quickly put their thoughts on paper. Explain that spelling is not important at this stage; instead meaning and clarity should be focussed on. Children 'have a go' at correct spelling. Stories may not be completed, depending on the individual's writing.

Editing

Parents read their story to their child. As families listen to the story, ask them to consider, "Is there anything I'd like to change, add, take out?" "Does the story say what I'd like it to say?" The child reads his/her story to the parent. The focus during the editing process is always on meaning. Parents are not to point out spelling or grammatical errors.

Revising

This part of the process may be done for homework. Parents and children now consider the mechanics of writing, spelling, punctuation, and grammar. As the stories are to be read by an audience, corrections are necessary.

Publishing

Stories may be sent in and displayed in the classroom, or shared at the next Language Partners evening.

Questions

Ask parents how they felt about the writing process. Did it help to focus and expand their writing? Explain that children do not edit and publish all story drafts. Students might do these stages once a month, for every fifth story, and so on. The students will have many opportunities to practise writing, create drafts, and revise meaning. The parents serve the same role in Language Partners as students or teachers in the classroom. Students need opportunities throughout the writing process to talk about and plan their story. Students can use the writing process for both fiction and nonfiction content.

Evening Five — Exploring Poetry

Prior to the evening, students and teachers may plan how they would like to share favorite poetry with parents. The selection offered may include student-written poetry and professional works. Ask students, in small groups, to choose one or two pieces to present. Final selections should include poems of varying mood and style.

The student groups may use Readers' Theatre techniques to plan their poetry presentation. Students can ask questions prior to commencing the activity in an effort to direct parents' attention during the reading.

Each group receives a poem to present. Students practice reciting the poem, and plan ways to deliver it in the most effective manner. Students collaborate, bearing in mind the mood, meaning of the poem, ways to vary voices (number, pace, loudness, pitch), and corresponding simple movements or dramatization. An alternative is for students to share the poems as in a poetry reading, where one student reads the chosen poem.

Each family writes down their last name. Together, parent and child create an acrostic poem. Each letter in the surname becomes the first letter in a word of a phrase representing the family.

e.g., S — portsmanlike
   T — alented
   E — ven-tempered
   V — oracious readers
   E — ager
   N — oble
   S — tudious
   O — rganized
   N — imble

Families might share these poems by reading them aloud, displaying them at their workplace, or on a bulletin board. Hopefully, the families will use this opportunity to reveal positive, humorous characteristics.

Each student or group of students can present their poetry selections to the parents and students. Following the reading/reciting, each family discusses the poem together, attempting to understand its meaning, and relate it to both adult and child's personal experiences. Key questions, generated by students or teachers, might be posted to direct parents' questioning.

Display a variety of poetry picture books, poetry anthologies, big books, and student work. Invite parents and children to choose a book and read some poetry together. Give each family a form with questions to consider before and after the reading. Questions might be:

"Read the title. Does it offer any ideas about the content of the poem. What do you think it will be about?"

"Look at any pictures. Do the illustrations offer a clue about the meaning of the poem?"

"Discuss together why we chose this poem."

"Read the poem together. What do you think this poem was about?"

"Did this poem remind you of a thing, a person, or an experience in your own lives?"

"How do you feel about this poem?"

"What is the mood of the poem? What did the poet write to create this mood?"

"What does the poem tell you about the poet? Why do you think s/he decided to write this poem?"

Explain to parents that offering shared poetry experiences allows at-risk readers to have reading experiences repeated in a safe, meaningful way.

Students' exposure to and writing of poetry offers opportunities for reflection, careful consideration of language and meaning, and exploration of human values.

Homework

Families might find a favorite piece of poetry to send to the class or share at the next Language Partners evening. Also, parents or students can write individual or collaborative poems to share with others. Because of this theme's popularity, it may take two evenings.

Evening Six — Yes, You Can Add in Writing

Openers

Ask the parents and children to think of two sentences that could start a story, for example, "My world started to spin before me as I hurtled through space. Was this a dream, or the real thing?" Ask the participants to brainstorm ideas that will continue the story.

Pre-Writing

Have the parents and children divide in to groups of four — two adults and two children. They discuss, in their groups, the direction their story will assume, as well as its tone — humorous, frightening, or sad.

First Draft

Give the groups ten minutes to record their story. As stated previously, remind everyone that spelling is not an issue at this stage of the writing process. Rather, the focus should be on the story development. Writing on every second line allows for later additions/deletions. Does it work? Is there a consistency to the story? Does it capture interest?

Editing

The groups can review their initial effort and determine what needs to be modified or changed in order to enhance the story. Once they have edited their story, provide time for the creation of accompanying illustrations. For ease of preparation, you might confine the choice of medium to crayons or markers as paints can be more time consuming.

Publishing

Have the groups present their illustrated stories to the others. It should be interesting to contrast what direction the groups have taken with their stories, given that they started with the same opening sentences.

Homework

A possible exercise for parents and children to do at home would be to select one story that was presented during the evening. Record the last two lines and compose a story at that takes off from the ''finished' story.

Evening Seven — Potatoes

Hall Activities

Venn Diagram

My Potato is

small
medium
round

Large   Oval
         Shaped

Bar Graph (choose one only)

Boiled	Baked	Mashed	French Fried	Home Fries	Scalloped	Potato Pancakes	Potato Salad	etc.

Large Potato Activity

For this activity, you will need thin, black markers, cut-out potato shapes, and masking tape. Participants can make the word "Potatoes" vertically as shown and list adjectives for each letter.

P Plump & pleasing
O Only underground
T Totally delicious
A Always a treat
T Tender when cooked
O Oven baked
E Everyone's favorite
S Sizzling in oil

Short Story

This is to be read by the parent and it leads into the Icebreaker. Our school's Irish principal read an Irish tale after the Icebreaker.

Icebreaker

Each person takes the name of one kind of cooked potato or a potato brand, for example, mashed potatoes, Idaho potatoes. Everyone moves around and introduces oneself (potato name) to another. They exchange potato names, move on to another person, and repeat the process. At the finish, ask volunteers to tell their original potato name and the one they ended up with.

Story — An Irish Tale

Each family's activity is as follows (on the previous evening each family was asked to bring in two interesting looking potatoes):

a) Look at both potatoes brought in. Choose the more interesting one, and then design an activity poster (a wanted poster) that features their potato. The picture can be in disguise. The description must be well detailed.

WANTED

Tristan and Mom.

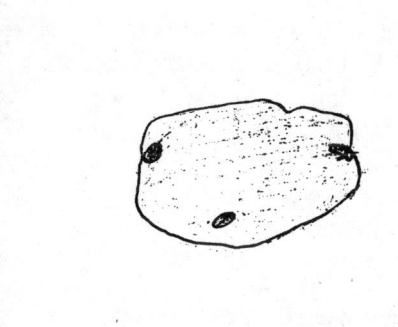

Flat top potatoe

Wanted by police.
The Crime — robbing Ban-dit.
oN Major street —Potatoe Lane
Beware—armed and dangerous.

If you spot Flat top Potatoe.
call 911 potatoe —immediat-ely.

REWARD $2,000,000 9

b) Each family places the interesting potato on a table in the center of the room. "Wanted" posters are collected and redistributed. When the family gets a new poster they look at the potato line-up and try to match the poster to the right potato. Some posters can be shared or a question asked to the group. for example, "What was the clue that helped the most?"

(The idea of a "Potato Wanted Poster" first appeared in the book *Student Centred Language Arts and Reading, K-13*, by James Moffett and Betty Jane Wagner, (Houghton Mifflin, 1983).)

Storyteller

We had a child tell the families a story.

Meaningful Memory

While Pat and Maureen were developing the Language Partners program, both arrived at the conclusion that they needed a visual representation of the program and its intent. The symbol below, decided on after some time and with a little help from a designer, aptly conveys the program's message and is used in all related workshops.

Language Partners Evaluation

The following form helps to evaluate the effectiveness of the Language Partners Program. Families fill out the evaluation form together so that it is a focus for reflection.

Language Partners Evaluation

Children and parents discuss the evaluation collaboratively.

We learned . . .

Due to our involvement in Language Partners we plan to . . .

Next time Language Partners is offered, we suggest . . .

Information to Share with Parents

These are handouts for parents explaining classroom programming and offering ideas for parents. Feel free to use all or parts of these with parents as you wish.

Questions Parents Ask

Please Remember:
Parents have the *right* to ask questions about their child's education. It reflects caring, and a need to understand the teaching/learning process. Well-informed, positive parents can serve as advocates and models within your school community.

Varied research states that positive parental involvement is the most significant factor contributing to children's school success. Parents are an underused resource available to support children's development and growth. Information about teaching and learning empowers parents to accept responsibility for influencing their child's success. As well, research has shown that teachers who gain parental support find their program easier to deliver.

Teachers have been exposed to new information and research about teaching and learning during the last fifteen years. Parents have not. They have only their own school experiences to use when evaluating and understanding good teaching practice. Educators must educate parents if we expect modern teaching methods to be positively received.

Honest, open responses from teachers develop a trusting relationship between educators and parents. Initially, the public views many of our institutions cynically and negatively. Educators need to actively work to reduce the barriers and create a trust between home and school.

It's alright to admit you don't know all the answers. Answer as honestly and informatively as you can about your beliefs and teaching practice. For those questions you can't answer, tell parents you will try to find out, like any good learner.

Questions may go beyond language issues. Recognize that parents need an opportunity to understand how the school functions and inquire about its educational beliefs and values.

Why does my child's teacher emphasize writing?

Writing is thought on paper. Writing reveals the writers' knowledge, understanding, and feelings about their world. Children's work combines the learning emphasis of the classroom and the writer's own interpretation of his/her own experiences. There is a correlation between frequent writing opportunities and children's reading development.

Writing requires a child to be personally engaged in his/her learning. When a child writes s/he is actively thinking, combining ideas, feelings, information, questions, and writing skills in a meaningful way.

Why does my child's teacher publish children's writing?

Children need to see their school work as relevant and meaningful (like adults in a work situation). Writing, to become meaningful, must have an audience. Publishing children's stories provides a reason for children to write their ideas and an audience for which to revise it. Published books become a source of learning and reading in classroom or school libraries.

Children also find audiences in other ways. Before, during, and after writing, children talk with others, both adults and peers, so they can plan, change, and share their writing. Opportunities to talk about their writing motivates children to improve the quality of their work, and acknowledges that learning is social in nature.

Why do children work in groups?

Children need opportunities to work in large and small groups, as well as in independent situations. Teachers consider the benefits of each kind of grouping situation and the organization that best suits the purpose of the learning activity.

The amount of work a child does in groups depends on the particular focus of a classroom. This may vary during the year.

Children are trained to work appropriately in group situations as this is a necessary skill in their present and future worlds.

Group work acknowledges that learning is social in nature. Ask parents to imagine a workplace where no discussion, planning, or sharing of information was allowed between coworkers. A classroom without group work does not take advantage of what is known about the nature of people and learning.

Why do educators encourage children to use invented spelling (approximations)?

To become competent writers and readers, children must be willing to take risks and write with confidence. Young writers need countless opportunities to explore and practise writing. Invented spelling (nonconventional spelling) does two things. It requires children, not adults, to do the thinking about what they know about writing and sound and letter relationships, and it empowers children to write independently.

The parents' and teachers' roles are to provide varied writing materials, relevant reasons to write, and audiences for writing.

Once students are competent, free writers, they can be taught to spell commonly used words found in their own writing or in themes within the classroom. Teachers take advantage of opportunities presented in students' writing to teach spelling in the context of the piece. Older students are encouraged to use invented spelling of difficult words during the first draft of their writing. This frees students to think about their ideas and to clarify their thinking, the real objective of writing. Students will revise grammar and spelling in some student or teacher selected pieces of writing throughout the year.

What kind of reading materials will my child use in school?

Your child reads a variety of materials within the classroom. Today's classrooms are filled with fiction, nonfiction materials, newspapers, poetry, magazines, children's published books, basal readers, and so on. The intent of a classroom filled with reading material is to promote reading. The kind of reading materials your child will use depends upon the classroom organization (e.g., time to read independently), and the focus of the learning during the classroom. If children are learning about whales, the reading children do should be around the sea and what not. Teachers collect a variety of different kinds and levels of writing to support classroom themes.

Why do teachers encourage talking?

Oral language between two or more people provides a means of communication and thinking. Talk allows children to problem solve, understand, analyze, question, predict, and gain and share knowledge in a classroom setting. Talking does not validate inappropriate behavior. Students, in a classroom where talk is accepted and valued, are less likely to create discipline problems.

Why do teachers encourage problem solving?

Children and adults, as part of a democracy, need to be able to rationally consider their decisions, and the ramifications of decisions on their lives. Problem solvers are alert, thoughtful learners who apply their knowledge to different situations. It is the teacher's role to put learning into the context of a problem or questions so students can approach learning in this way. The ability to problem solve and make decisions has been identified by business and government institutions as one of the most crucial skills for the 21st century.

What do educators mean by Whole Language?

Whole Language refers to a teaching philosophy that emphasizes ideas being presented initially as a whole. From this larger context, the ideas and materials move into a narrower focus. As an example, a complete story is read to/with children depending on their abilities. Teachers draw out students' prior knowledge, questions, and personal interpretations before, during, and after the reading of the text. Students talk, listen, write, and read other support material to deepen the reading experience for the students. The structures of language are taught within the context of the learning experience, not in isolation and to students who require it. It is not necessary to teach children something they already know. The teacher's role is to know his/her children well enough to determine what they know and what they need to know. Individual, small group, and whole class instruction grows out of the teacher's diagnosis of student needs.

Make Language Partners a Summer Program

Summer is the perfect time to practise together the language skills and strategies your child has acquired in school. Reading, like music lessons or baseball, needs to be reinforced through direct involvement.

There are many activities that you and your child can enjoy together. Chat about all the options out there within your community and extended world. Listen to each other! Choose your favorite activities and savor every minute. Remember to laugh a lot, and take photos. Try some of these cooperative adventures.

A Time Capsule

This can be started at any age. Choose a suitable large container that your child might enjoy decorating. Decide where it will be stored. Discuss the type of articles you want put in it each summer and how many (3, 4, 5?) articles will represent each family member.

Enter a successful piece of writing or drawing from a younger child to profile your child's growth. Invite your child to label the item with yellow stickies. S/he might state the relevance of the article, date, and so on. Remember, as parents it is important to look for meaningful opportunities to encourage your child to write.

One woman sent each of her children a letter on his/her birthday telling of her love and pride in the child's development and strengths. This could be a perfect item to add. This venture could be a special secret shared between two or all family members.

Going Places

The expanse of summer offers parents and children opportunities to explore both their community and attractions farther afield. Outings with children need to have certain components in place to ensure parental survival (and enjoyment). Visiting attractions with children also need to be acknowledged as a very strong learning experience.

Though these statements seem obvious, we have observed parents during an outing, either silent or talking with their child about totally different issues. This kind of parenting situation does not take advantage of the potential learning possible. Another kind of parent treats his/her child like an equal, and does not set limits for the child. Both frustrated parent and confused child are not smiling too much at the end of the experience.

When interacting with your child, there are two different hats a parent will wear to come home smiling. There needs to be a balance between these two roles. The styles will interchange during the course of the event as situations evolve. Remind yourself that it is necessary to strike a balance between parenting behavior and interactive behavior.

Parenting Behavior

1. Limits (appropriate for whatever age) must be established first. As an example, "You have seven dollars to spend on souvenirs or games. You will need to decide how that may be spent during the day."
2. Explain your general expectations for the day (safety, basic manners towards everyone in the group).
3. Talk about what you would like to get out of the day. It is our job as parents to help children understand that we also have needs, and it is important that they be accommodated. If children do not begin to learn this gradually, we make their present and future relationships more difficult. Through negotiation, help your child see himself/herself as having individual rights while at the same time being part of a group.
4. Establish a place to meet in case someone gets lost. Remind younger (and older) children to go to the washroom with a buddy.
5. Talk about a tentative time you will eat. Children seem to think about eating as soon as you arrive anywhere.

Discussions based on topics as those given above help children understand the format of the day and give them comfort.

Interactive Behavior

1. Draw your child's attention to the features of the experience/event.
2. Promote problem solving and decision making throughout the day. If appropriate, talk about the decisions that the people

responsible for creating, planning, and/or running the event face. This helps your child to understand different points of view, perspectives, and project ideas.

3. Give information casually and incidentally in a pleasant voice.
4. Use conversation to stimulate more questions and discussion.
5. Compare the outing to others you have taken or plan to take. Evaluate the outing with your child at the end of the experience. "What did you like best?" "Would you recommend this to your friends?" Why?" "What did you find most fun/interesting?"
6. Understand that the event may result in an extension (reading a related book, researching a question that arose) after the event.

Experiences are Important

Experiences can enhance your child's comprehension in reading, listening, and viewing. If your child learns to sail, s/he hears the language of sailing (nautical terms), understands the broader concepts of sailing (anticipating winds, the relationship of wind to the sail), and the social context and ritual of sailing. S/he has been involved in a learning experience that is relevant and directly applicable (you learn the rudiments of sailing through sailing, practising, listening to others, reading manuals, etc.).

The effect of experience on a child's understanding of literature or nonfiction material may be this: if your child either selects or is asked to read a book involving a sailing experience s/he brings prior knowledge to the text. S/he can recognize the pronunciation of the words due to hearing/using them previously. Difficult vocabulary and images have meaning to the student due to his/her past experiences.

Vacation Planning

- Write a letter to or phone the Chamber of Commerce or Department of Tourism for information on areas of interest.
- Do research at your local library on all the places to visit.
- Keep a log of your trip.
- Map out the route.
- Take photos, label them, and write a story.
- Send a postcard to friends and family at home.

- Make a mini-comic book of your vacation.
- Place words in the "bubbles" above the characters' heads.
- Search out the newspaper in your vacation spot.
- Compare them to those at home.
- Try some shared reading, especially the comics.
- If you visit an old village, town, or city casually interview the manager of a hotel/motel/inn about the history of the building and the environs. Real moments with history help children to understand the past when they meet it in school.

At Home and in the Community

Encourage your child to play school and be creative.

Visit your local library and find out about summer programs. Our local library offers incentive reading challenges, videos, movies, puppet shows, community visitory, storytelling, and collaborative cooking. These are all legitimate learning experiences that foster growth.

Establish a neighborhood adult/child Book Club among your friends. Share things like your favorite part of a story, references to other similar books, and personal experiences triggered by the text of the book. Find other books by the same author, sketch a part of the book or its characters, create a dramatization or puppet play, tape record a funny part of the book, play it at the meeting, or just read a part you enjoyed. Bring along a favorite photo from the summer and tell about it. Have a poetry afternoon. Share a music tape. Read to a 'little' neighbor, your favorite toy, a pet, even a family plant.

Read along with the tape of the same story.

Try out a new hobby and research it at the library or the local bookstore. Try to find someone locally who has some expertise and learn from them. Ask for some tips.

Plan a simple sidewalk sale of outgrown toys and books. Organize the tables and money float and make signs. Plan a lemonade/popcorn booth. Send out invitations to your friends and neighbors.

Make a list of your favorite summer foods. How many ice cream flavors can you think of?

Find a quiet spot by a shady tree and read your book while someone else reads their book.

Visit a neighborhood seniors' home and read to an elderly person.

Make a personal time line, highlighting the main events in your child's (or family's) life.

Language Learning with Your Child: Suggestions for Parents

Active Listening

Read a story aloud and purposely make silly errors or mispronounce a familiar word while reading. Your child will become very alert and seek meaning from what you are reading.

Encourage your child to acquire some taped books, stories, and music.

Collaborative Thinking/Talking/Problem Solving/Drama

Extend your child's understanding of the world by informally sharing with him/her your knowledge of an experience, event, or situation. Help him/her to understand different points of view, make inferences about situations, compare events to past experiences, and look for alternative ideas.

Ask your child to make up a story at bedtime. Ask what is the problem in the story, where it will take place, who will be in it, and so on. Create a story on the spot. A story created together let's everyone feel closer and more clever.

Share the meaning of more sophisticated language with your child in an informal way. This helps a student understand it when s/he sees it in print.

Encourage brainstorming/discussions around statements that interest individual family members. Promote and allow sharing of thoughts.

Involve your child in planning an event, for example, making decisions about decorating a table for a birthday dinner. Let him/her make the decisions without your involvement if possible.

Model aloud your thinking. Let your child see how you make decisions and solve simple problems every day.

Buy games like "Scrabble", "Password", and "Wheel of Fortune" to help spelling and language acquisition.

Purposeful Reading

Invest in a set of magnetic letters for the refrigerator. Encourage your child to play with the letters, and try new and familiar words.

An early reader benefits from listening to taped stories. Tape favorite stories. Read very slowly to allow your child to look for picture clues, and match your voice with the print. Help your child to re-read selections with some fluency.

Schedule a reading time for your family. Bedtime is usually the most convenient and calm. An older child can read independently for half an hour, and a younger child can read with you. Make this routine calm, consistent, and enjoyable.

Early readers find success with nursery rhymes, and predictable and pattern books. When reading, allow children to fill in words and phrases they anticipate.

Expose your child to nonfiction material, newspaper articles, nature magazines, books, and so on. Help him/her to read and understand factual material.

Ask your child to help you follow a simple recipe. S/he will love to read the directions, stir, and lick the bowl.

Begin a story. Ask your child to add the next section. Continue the story until it is exhausted.

Before reading with your child, ask questions to stimulate prediction of the story/information. During the story, discuss pictures, dialogue, humor, and so on. Remember, the more pleasurable you make the reading experience, the more your child will be attracted to it.

After reading with your child, try to engage him/her in a relaxed discussion about the book. Your child might retell the story, relate it to his/her own experiences, or create a conversation in role as one of the characters.

If English is your second language, read to your child in your first language. A child who is read to acquires other languages more easily.

Expose your child to the many forms of print in our world — maps, brochures, newspapers, timetables, recipes, messages, letters, signs. Point out the different forms writing takes in our environment and read them with/to him/her.

Identify your child's favorite authors and genres of books. Keep your child's interest up by giving these as gifts, and talking about books.

Meaningful Writing

Seek opportunities for your child to write for a purpose, for example, write a letter to a relative or leave a note on a message board. The more opportunities your child has to write freely and usefully in different forms, the greater his/her growth.

Purchase a whiteboard or blackboard for your child to practice writing. Use this board to communicate information for your family.

Invest in lots of paper for drawing and writing. Encourage your child to draw and practice writing frequently. Offer different media for writing, for example: large felt pens, crayons, thin markers, pens, and so on.

Listen to your child read his/her stories to you. Accept the stories, and look past the spelling for the meaning. Try to comment on the clarity of thought expressed, not the errors. Your child will not be practicing formal spelling until s/he is an established reader (about grade three). Encourage your child to take a risk when writing a first draft story. Help him/her to focus on the meaning, choice of language, and mood.

Encourage your child to keep a diary or calendar each year. These serve as vehicles to promote writing and to reflect on change during the year. Younger children can draw pictures of important events.

Purchase a thesaurus to offer alternative language for children.

Have a dictionary available, but never ask children to look up a word in the dictionary if they are unable to read it in a book. Give them the word so the meaning of the text is not disrupted and allow them to continue. Pictionaries and theme dictionaries are best for early readers.

Model/write a story for your child. Let him/her see and hear your process and how you make changes when choosing words as you create the story. Ask your child for suggestions if you wrote a story together.

Keep a sample of your child's writing each year. S/he will appreciate looking back on his/her work and recognizing the growth.

Write out favorite songs and allow your child to read along as s/he sings.

Offer your child an opportunity to express his/her own thoughts and views using a scrapbook, developing a collection, personalizing a cartoon form, and so on.

Foster drama opportunities — role playing around shared stories, creating conversations where parent and child become book characters, interviewing each other and engaging in dramatic play.

Directed Viewing

Share in the selection and discuss television shows you are watching. Let your child hear your point of view. Allow him/her to share thoughts with you.

Attend as many family-type plays and movies together as possible. Use these experiences as a springboard for discussion.

Use sports events to promote discussion, predicting, and so on.

Learning Behaviors

Help your child feel successful. Talk about growing up, goal setting, and imaging his/her future life. This helps your child to visualize a positive future direction.

Be reasonable but clear about what constitutes appropriate family behavior.

Set high expectations for learning and listening in school. Your child will model the importance s/he sees you put on formal schooling.

Enjoy your child. Laugh and look for the good.

Needs of Children

AT HOME, CHILDREN NEED . . .	AT SCHOOL, CHILDREN NEED . . .
opportunities to practise and apply what they're learning;	opportunities to practise and apply what they're learning;
to be understood and accepted throughout their developmental stages;	to be understood and accepted throughout their developmental stages;
to be accepted for their uniqueness and strengths;	to be accepted for their uniqueness and strengths;
to be exposed to literature by being read to daily;	to be exposed to literature by being read to daily;
to have their various successes celebrated, including academic, both formally and informally;	to have their various successes celebrated, including academic, both formally and informally;
to have opportunities for quiet reflection;	to have opportunities for quiet reflection;
to be told they are loved without conditions;	to be told they're liked without conditions;
to be allowed to take guided, appropriate risks;	to be allowed to take guided, appropriate risks;
to be given appropriate responsibilities and consequences;	to be given appropriate responsibilities and consequences;
to have their learning styles recognized and accommodated;	to have their learning styles recognized and accommodated;
to have frequent opportunities to work collaboratively and develop friendships.	to have frequent opportunities to work collaboratively and develop friendships.

HOPED FOR OUTCOME — CARING, INDEPENDENT, CONFIDENT HAPPY ADULTS

Children who are utilizing their potential . . .

are read to;
are confident, feel good about themselves;
are risk-takers;
see themselves as learners and understand their role in learning;
have goals;
seek help if they need it from peers, teachers, other adults;
are well-rested and nourished;
exhibit self-control;
accept failure as a part of learning;
accept responsibility;
are attentive listeners;
cultivate good manners.

Ways to Help Your Child Do Well in School

A-sk what went well at school each day and what s/he is involved in. Be positive about your approach.

B-e sure to enjoy many experiences together because out of doing comes learning.

C-elebrate your child's special strengths and skills, and continue to find ways to help your child be the best that s/he can be.

D-evelop your child's social skills by allowing him/her to have many experiences with many different people. Support informal playtime as it is important, too.

E-ncourage your child to take responsibility for his/her own behavior, schoolwork, and homework.

F-orget adult concerns when communicating with your child.

G-ive your child consistent expectations and support around homework. Establish a designated time and place for homework to be done.

H-ug your child often — at least three times a day. Older children need to be hugged and touched as well, but timing is everything.

I-nstill your child with a sense of routine around bedtime. Active, growing children need lots of sleep.

J-ump for joy with the knowledge that you and your family are the most important people in your child's life. It is your values and strengths that your child will imitate.

K-eep your child adequately nourished. Start each day with a smile and a good breakfast.

L-isten when your child has a problem. Enlist his/her participation in the solution.

M-odel a sense of humor for your child. It will always serve him/her well.

N-otice when your child does a job well, and dresses neatly and appropriately for the weather.

O-ffer your child opportunities to make simple decisions. These decisions will become more frequent and more sophisticated as the child gets older.

P-ut your child's successful work up somewhere in the house for all to enjoy.

Q-uestion your child's teacher and/or coaches often about how your child is doing in the classroom and/or on the team.

R-ead to your child regularly, and let your child see you reading appropriate material. Show your interest and support and write together, too.

S-ee that your child gets regular physical activity. Help him/her establish a sense of fitness for life.

T-each your child good manners, how to respond to and behave in social situations. This will create security in your child.

U-nderstand that your child will make mistakes along the way. We learn from our mistakes and mature through them.

V-olunteer to participate at your child's school whenever you can. This demonstrates to your child that school is an important place.

W-atch TV and videos with your child. Talk about what you watch together. Encourage limited, selective watching.

EX-pect your child to try to do his/her best. Encourage quality work and ongoing effort.

Y-ou can help your child to understand and cope with real life issues if you provide him/her with honest answers to questions.

Z-oom forward along life's pathways with zest and zeal. Life is an adventure.

The authors would like to acknowledge the contribution of Glenys McCreath to the development of these pages.

The Writing Process

Our students follow a sequence of tasks beginning with the student selection of a topic, through revision, and ending with a polished, finished piece of writing.

Students have individual writing folders. Pieces of student writing, representing the draft stage, finished products, and a variety of forms of writing are collected throughout the year. These folders provide teachers, parents, and students with information on students' development in writing over time. They help the teacher and student to identify areas to focus on in the future.

This process is based on the idiosyncratic process all authors use during writing. We have outlined it here, along with teacher/parent ideas to support/extend each stage. Our students are trained to know the writing process steps — different students will be at various stages during our writing time.

STAGE	CHILD'S ROLE	TEACHER/PARENT ROLE
Pre-writing Ideas and topics are narrowed down to create a story focus.	Students plan, compare, think, question, act out, and rehearse their story ideas.	Adult stimulates thinking around an experience or ideas through discussion, role playing, listening to poetry, viewing a film.

This stage is usually done in class. Students are encouraged to share their own ideas and listen to others to develop their stories. Opportunities to talk and discuss provide the basis for the students' developing story structure. The topics selected usually reflect and expand students' individual knowledge and experiences.

Writing The first draft is an attempt to get thoughts on paper.	Students write quickly, concentrating on ideas and meaning, not spelling and punctuation.	Adult encourages risk-taking and guessing. "Write the words as best you can." First drafts might be shared aloud, listening for rich images, point of view.

This stage can be done during class or as a homework assignment. Students write on one side of a paper, every second line to encourage future revisions. Erasers are not encouraged; instead students are encouraged to guess correct spelling of difficult words. Students will have daily opportunities to write.

Revising

The writer, often with the help of others (teachers or students) rereads the piece of writing, focussing on content, and improving the quality. The writing is the task.

Students add, delete, change ideas and language, focussing on meaning.

"Would you like to add anything to your story?" "Did you mean . . . ?" "Could you describe your character more fully?" "What was the character thinking?"

All pieces of student writing will not be revised. Students may choose to revise a piece of writing monthly or after five draft pieces. Students decide which piece of writing they would like to improve. Students in grades one and two will do little revision as they cannot recognize the need to change their stories.

Editing

Student writing to be presented to an audience requires correct spelling and punctuation. Edited writing provides models for other writers.

Students rewrite their draft, creating a polished product.

Teacher works with students on the mechanics of writing. S/he uses the writing as a teaching tool acknowledging what s/he has learned and teaching new skills.

Publishing

Writing becomes relevant to students when they have the opportunity to read their work to other audiences. Students listen to appreciate the quality of the writing.

Students read their work to individuals, small or large groups. Writing may be displayed throughout the school and classroom.

Adults receive the finished writing positively. Teachers help student see themselves as part of a "community of writers", always working to improve their product.

Note:
Some writing will be private and will not be shared with others.

If You Don't Know a Word . . .

Early readers need to develop strategies for unlocking unknown words. This chart can be kept in children's rooms or wherever reading might take place. Refer to the chart whenever a reader becomes stuck on a word. The more often children try this strategy with success, the greater the chance of their using it independently.

What do you do if you don't know a word . . .
go back to the beginning of the sentence.
start again.
say the beginning sound.
take a guess.

If you're still stuck . . .
go back to the beginning of the sentence.
read again.
read to the end of the sentence.
take a guess and think about . . . does this make sense?

You can also . . .
look for picture clues.
look for little words inside big words.
look for sounds you know.

Reading Aloud

Reading aloud to children facilitates the growth of lifelong literacy skills. Experiences with books promote the development of the following skills and knowledge.

Children learn:

to become good listeners;
to lengthen their attention spans;
to see books as a relevant part of their lives;
to extend their oral vocabulary;
to understand higher level vocabulary when they meet it in print;
to recognize different styles of narrative writing;
to gain information about their world and its relationship to their lives;
to derive pleasure from literature;

to value reading as they see their parents do;

to build up a sight vocabulary;

to use literature as a springboard for expressing opinions and developing critical thinking;

to use literature to develop an understanding of other times, places, and points of view;

to hear adult readers model expression and fluency;

to understand that writers adapt language to suit different purposes;

to understand the differences between spoken and written language;

to understand that elements of story exist — setting, characters, problem resolution;

to recognize the link between literature and illustrations;

to use pictures to extend the story meaning;

to understand that writing comes in different forms — poetry, short stories, chapter books, nonfiction;

to develop personal taste in genres of reading — science fiction, historical fiction, etc.;

to allow books to provide a link of common experience with parents;

to see themselves as readers.

A Parent's Guide to Reading

Before Reading

Look at the Cover:
What do you think this book will be about?

Look at the Author's Name:
Have we read any other books by this author?
Is there any information on the back about the author?

Look at the Parts of the Book:
— dedication
— contents
— publication

While Reading

Questions to Assess Understanding:
What do you think silent means?

Questions to Link Child's Experience:
Have you ever seen a live turtle?

Questions to Compare:
How is your home different from this one?

Questions to Relate:
Do you like this character? Why/why not?

Questions to Predict:
What do you think will happen?

Questions to Guide Observation:
What is happening in the picture?

After Reading

Questions to Evaluate:
What did you like about this story?
What did you not like?
What was this story about?
What was your favorite part?

The authors would like to acknowledge Glenys McCreath's contribution to the development of this page.

Stages of Reading Development

Observe your child, listen to him/her read, and talk to his/her teacher to determine your child's stage in reading development.

Emergent Reader

Characteristics of an Emergent Reader

- likes to be read to;
- enjoys having stories re-read;
- understands that stories have meaning;
- looks at the picture for meaning;
- pretends to "read" favorite stories, relying on memory and picture clues;
- plays with language (enjoys nonsense rhymes, etc.);
- near the end of this stage may recognize that certain words begin with certain sounds;
- expects to meet success in reading;
- recognizes his/her own name and may print it;
- recognizes some written words in his/her "world", for example, restaurant signs, labels, road signs.

Suggestions for Adult Support

- read *daily* (books with patterns, fairy tales, rhyming poetry, predictable endings, picture books);
- allow child to select bedtime story;
- agree to re-read stories as often as child wants;
- encourage child to fill in predictable and familiar words;
- discuss the picture;
- listen to reading and accept positively;
- talk to your child about "becoming a reader";
- incidentally draw child's attention to letters, letter sounds if child is listening;
- offer child alphabet letters to handle;
- recognize this stage as a valid one and the basis for the next stage;
- offer taped stories as another option to allow your child to hear stories independently, repetitively, and frequently;
- in a positive, incidental relevant way begin to direct child's attention to words around him/her, for example, "Tell me when I come to the restaurant sign, so I will know when to stop."

- clearly demonstrate to your child that you value reading;
- if English is your second language, read to your child in the language you are most proficient in.

Characteristics of an Early Reader

- still looks for meaning in print;
- tries to match the words on the page;
- finger points;
- reads slowly and deliberately;
- reads orally rather than silently;
- begins to utilize his/her knowledge of the relationship between common letters and sounds;
- focuses directly on individual words, but can use picture clues, re-reading a sentence to maintain meaning;
- reads familiar, predictable material independently at the end of this stage;
- has a basic sight vocabulary developed from personal reading;
- understands the need for independent application in order to develop reading proficiency.

Suggestions for Adult Support

- help your child envision himself/herself as a reader;
- provide a setting full of books, offering predictable literature, stories incorporating child's basic vocabulary;
- be an audience for your child to read to;
- offer ongoing opportunities for your child to re-read and practise familiar material;
- continue to read aloud to your child, as your reading offers him a model of fluent, expressive reading and a source of literary and technical knowledge;
- informally and incidentally draw your child's attention to the structure of a word;
- allow your child to select stories to be read aloud and to develop a sense of individual taste in stories;
- tape stories, *reading very slowly*, to allow a child to follow along in the book and look to make a voice/print match;
- try shared reading, a child reads familiar words and you read any words s/he cannot figure out;
- provide ongoing, frequent, relevant writing opportunities;
- encourage invented (approximation) spelling as this helps your child to think independently about sound/symbol relationships

and his/her understanding of written language;

- engage your child in conversation about a story — before, during, and after reading;
- demonstrate that you read, and that you value reading;
- teach the steps to *If You Don't Know a Word*;
- recognize and celebrate growth in reading;
- promote positive reading experiences.

Fluent Reader

Characteristics of a Fluent Reader

- sees himself/herself as a successful reader;
- reads a variety of materials (nonfiction, fiction magazines, newspapers) both at home and at school;
- reads silently, skims and scans to suit his/her purpose;
- recognizes that writers have biases, points of view that drive their writing;
- can identify writers' perspectives and relate this to his/her own experiences;
- reads aloud with expression;
- displays comprehension through discussion, re-telling the story, drawing;
- appreciates writing styles and may develop favorite genres or styles;
- may be a confident writer, developing his/her own style;
- is able to draw information from text, note-take, jot down information;
- recognizes the various formats books have, for example: chapters, bibliography, index.

Suggestions for Adult Support

- engage your child in discussions about the theme of an article, or a book;
- offer your child frequent opportunities to visit the school and local library;
- continue to read aloud — poetry, fiction, newspaper articles;
- look for opportunities to refer to current events and the issues surrounding them, dialogue with your child about your point of view, help your child articulate his/her perspective;
- model that you value reading and read yourself;

- identify your child's favorite authors, preferred genres of books, and nonfiction interests, and look for opportunities (birthdays etc.) to present books, magazines to your child;
- celebrate verbally your child's development as a reader;
- encourage opportunities for your child to read independently for sustained periods.

Stages of Spelling/Writing

Your child will progress through the stages in spelling/writing as s/he develops greater understanding of written language. Consider the kind of writing your child is currently doing, identify his/her stage, and attempt to support his/her development. As you read samples of your child's writing, look for evidence of what your child *does know* about writing/spelling rather than what your child *does not know*. Focus on the positive when talking with your child about his/her development. Expect your child to progress. Keep dated samples of your child's development in writing. Point out to your child all that s/he has learned.

Stage	Adult Support
Scribble or Random Letters • lines, circles, waves on paper, letters unrelated to sounds in words • child "reads" story • story may change meaning with each retelling	• encourage writing and receive beginning writing positively • offer access to writing materials, such as paper, markers, white board, chalkboard • model writing, talk about what you are writing and why you are writing it • supply alphabet letters for the fridge
Initial Consonants • child writes beginning sounds of letters to represent a word • spacing between words may appear	• draw child's attention to *sounds* of letters rather than focus on letter names • continue to show your child you value his/her developing writing skills • talk about what you see him/her *able to do* • if your child questions you about writing, letter sounds, and word meanings take time to answer and explain the whole concept, give examples s/he can relate to

Stage	Adult Support
Final Consonants • child writes beginning and final consonant sounds	• Model writing and talk about what you are doing and why • talk about spaces between words, left to right directionality • comment on the *thought* in the writing, *not spelling at this stage*
Consonants in Middle of Words	• draw your child's attention to his/her approximation and standard spelling. Notice what s/he spelled correctly. • correction of writing discourages the writer
Vowels Begin *Over Generalization of Patterns* • child spells words without understanding of exceptions to rules	• encourage risk taking when writing • may begin editing of writing after revising meaning • talk about spelling patterns, for example, rhyming words • discuss the meaning of root words incidentally • continue to identify and use writing opportunities, for example: thank you notes, pen pals, birthday cards, shopping lists
Growing Awareness of Rules and Exceptions	• teach him/her to use a simple dictionary, thesaurus • continue to look for the meaning in the writing before spelling, grammar • talk about and point out different forms of writing and their components • look for audiences for your child's writing • continue to offer your child many different writing experiences • the purpose of writing should determine the form • encourage chapter stories

Storybooks for Read-Aloud

This is a sample list of one teacher librarian's favorite storybooks. You might like to read some of these stories to/with your children.

Marian Teal's list of "Good Books"

1. *The Blue Faieine Hippotamus*
   Author — Joan Grant
   Illustrator — Alexander Day
   Publisher — The Green Tiger Press
   — Egyptian tale
   — good for storytelling
   — picture book

2. *The Little Prince*
   Author — Antoine de Saint Exupéry
   Published 1943
   Publisher — Harcourt Brace Jovanovich
   — French
   — fantasy
   — chapter book

3. *The Mountains of Tibet*
   Author — Mordecai Gerstein
   Published 1987
   Publisher — Harper and Row
   — Reincarnation theme
   — Tibet
   — picture book

4. *Grandfather Twilight*
   Author — Barbara Berger
   Published 1984
   Publisher Philomel Books (a division of Putnam and Grosset)
   — good for drama
   — picture book

5. *The Bunyip of Berkley's Creek*
   Author — Jenny Wagner
   Illustrator — Ron Brooks
   Publisher — Puffin Books
   — Australian
   — simple drama material
   — picture book

6. *The Orphan Boy*
   Author — Tololwa M. Mollel
   Illustrator — Paul Morin
   Published — 1990
   Publisher Oxford University Press
   — Masai
   — picture book

7. *Lon Po Po*
   Translated and illustrated by Ed Young
   Published 1989
   Publisher Philomel Books
   — A Red Riding Hood story from China
   — picture book

8. *Once Upon a Golden Apple*
   Author — Jean Little and Maggie De Vries
   Illustrator — Phoebe Gilman
   — good for language extension
   — picture book

Published — 1991
Publisher — Viking Child

9. *The Dancing Tigers*   — Indian tale
   Author — Russel Hoban and   — picture book
      David Gentleman
   Published — 1983
   Publisher — Jonathan Cape, London

10. *The Weaving of a Dream*   — Chinese tale
    Author — Marilee Heyer   — picture book
    Published — 1986
    Publisher — Viking Kestrel

11. *The Great Kapok Tree*   — tale of the Amazon
    Author — Lynne Cherry   Rain Forest
    Published 1990   — picture book
    Publisher — Harcourt Brace
    Jovanovich

12. *The Most Beautiful Place in the*   — Guatemalan
    World   — beginning chapter
    Author — Ann Cameron   book
    Illustrator — Thomas Allen
    Published — 1988
    Publisher — Knopf, New York

13. *The Name of the Tree*   — Bantu tale
    Retold by — Celia Lottridge   — picture book
    Illustrator — Ian Wallace
    Published — 1989
    Publisher — Groundwood Books

14. *Mufaro's Beautiful Daughters*   — African tale
    Author — John Steptoe   — picture book
    Publisher — Lothrup Lee and
    Shephard, New York

15. *The Painter and the Wild Swans*   — picture book
    Author — Claude Clement
    Illustrator — Frederic Clement
    Published — 1989
    Publisher — Dial Books

16. *Miss Rumphius*   — picture book
    Author — Barbara Cooney
    Published — 1982
    Publisher — Puffin Books, Viking
    Press

17. *The Silver Cow*   — Welsh tale
    Retold by Susan Cooper   — picture book
    Illustrator Warwick Hutton
    Published — 1983
    Publisher — Collier MacMillan

18. *The Banza*   — Haitian story
    Author — Diane Wolkstein   — picture book
    Illustrator — Mari Brown
    Published — 1981
    Publisher — Dial Press

19. *Keepers of the Earth*   — Native stories
    Authors — Michael J. Caduto   — environmental activ-
      and Joseph Bruchee   ities for children
    Illustrators — J. Fedden and Carol
      Wood
    Publishers — Fifth House Publishers

20. *The Day of Ahmed's Secret*   — boy's story set in
    Author — Florence Heide and   Cairo, Egypt
      Judith Gilliland
    Illustrator — Ted Lewin
    Published — 1990
    Publisher — Lothrop Lee and Shepard
    Books

Posing Questions for Children

Questions to Model

Helping Children Learn to Ask

What
What would you do?
What would you have done?
What name would you give to . . .?
What change(s) do you see? suggest?
What did s/he say about?
What will happen next . . .?

Where
Where would you go to see . . .?
Where could you find . . .?

How
How could you make it work?
How does it work?
How could you go about . . .?

When
When will it happen?
When could you . . .?
When could you see . . .?

Who
To whom could you write?
Who would you call, speak to, ask, see, invite to . . .?
Who could help?
Who knows about. . .?

Why
Why does it do that?
Why did you add this to . . .? place this here . . . ? put this
. . . ?

The authors would like to acknowledge the contribution of Glenys McCreath to the development of this page.

Today's Child in Tomorrow's World

As we move into the 21st century, educators and parents need to thoughtfully envision the kinds of skills, behaviors, and values our children will need in order to function successfully in the future. If we determine what kind of "products" we are working to create in our schools and in our homes, based on what children will need, then the kinds of experiences our students *should* have become more clear. Parents and educators in each school might want to identify *their* views around this question. We believe children will need *practice* during their childhoods to develop:

- critical thinking and problem solving skills;
- strong skills in all communication modes (oral and written), and in science and math;
- the ability to function in a multiculturally diverse democratic society;
- the ability to be a productive worker, committing energy towards quality and service;
- a striving for and recognition of excellence;
- an awareness of the fragility of the environment;
- an appreciation of aesthetic through experiences with art and music;
- comfort with technology;
- the ability to access information;
- positive attitudes towards preventative health and physical fitness;
- social responsibilities;
- confidence to accept responsibility for their own decisions;
- positive values within a complex, evolving world.

By strengthening our partnership between home and school, we create a safety net of success for children, and strong support that will guide them throughout their childhood and adolescence. Our collaborative efforts should help children to be well equipped to enter the next century with self-assurance and anticipation.

Appendix

This curriculum statement was developed by teachers of each grade level at Queen Victoria Public School as a result of a teacher workshop (see pg. 15) in order to describe the basic elements of "what is taught" at the school.

It is important that we focus on children as individuals, and provide for their physical, emotional, social, and intellectual development. To do this we must plan a program that will help our students to learn skills, acquire knowledge, and gain a sense of their own self-worth.

The curriculum, too, must be seen as a whole unit based on research about language development and learning theory. Themes are developed that integrate information from many subject areas. A wide variety of experiences and teaching strategies are used as a springboard to learning. Through observation, teachers identify and build on students' strengths and plan to work on areas of concern. Our school recognizes individual differences, teaching students at their identified levels using the most appropriate teaching method — whole class, small group, or individual instruction.

Language, Mathematics, Environmental Studies and the Arts are combined "in the Primary and Junior Divisions so that each (student) may pursue his or her education with satisfaction and share in the life of the community with competence, integrity and joy".[1]

These are the four language areas we chose to focus on: listening, speaking, reading and writing.

Listening: Skills such as comparing and interpreting sounds, recognizing language patterns, (e.g., rhymes), and following

---

[1] Education in the Primary and Junior Divisions, Ontario Ministry of Education

spoken directions are part of the primary focus (Kindergarten, Grades 1, 2, and 3).

At the junior level (Grades 4, 5, and 6) students are encouraged to listen to gain information, listen critically, and interpret what they hear. Students from all grades are invited to monthly assemblies to celebrate and share their work and interests.

Daily announcements using student speakers recognize students' successes, provide information, and establish common school goals. Classroom activities are structured to promote purposeful listening among individuals and small and large groups.

Speaking: In the primary grades students are helped to form clear ideas and master a vocabulary to explain and understand their world.

Older students are helped to expand and clarify their views through student discussion.

Teachers provide daily opportunities for oral language growth in a variety of ways, for example: problem solving, discussions, presentations.

Reading: Young children acquire reading skills in a variety of ways, for example: writing stories, learning word attack skills, reading pattern and predictable books, and using basal readers. These skills relate directly to the experiences of children.

In the junior grades more sophisticated skills such as predicting, analyzing, and comparing stories are emphasized, using a variety of reading materials.

Children's strengths are developed and weaknesses remediated by teaching children at their own reading level. The enjoyment and practical use of books is an important part of every grade. The staff is committed to reading good literature to students daily. Each class participates in a quiet reading period daily. Students select from a variety of reading material. All students enjoy regular access to books through school and neighborhood library visits.

To encourage parent involvement and regular oral reading opportunities, Home Reading programs have been introduced throughout the school. Primary children read regularly with others each night while junior students may read and discuss lengthier books at home.

Writing: Students write daily in a variety of ways for different purposes, for example: stories, poetry, letters, reports, and observations.

Spelling, handwriting, grammar, and punctuation skills are developed from students' individual writing abilities. Students focus on the writing process, that is, pre-writing experience, writing, editing, and final copy. The school provides a number of vehicles for the sharing of writing, for example: assemblies, published books, cross grade sharing.

Listening

Kindergarten

Activities are structured to develop students' listening skills. Teachers:

- provide listening centers with music, records, tapes, and read-along books;
- read a variety of books daily;
- encourage good listening through simple directions, consistent routines, and signals;
- have daily musical activities;
- provide opportunities for students to listen purposefully to each other in large and small groups, for example, conversations, sharing time.

Grade 1

The skill of listening is developed in a variety of ways. Teachers:

- provide students with opportunities to listen purposefully to one another;
- help students follow simple oral directions, routines, and signals,
- read a variety of books daily;
- help students focus their listening through questioning;
- ask students to repeat information, instructions, and stories.

Grade 2

Students listen for a variety of purposes, for example: to sequence events, find details, retell a story, follow specific directions, and for enjoyment. Teachers:

- give instructions with increasing complexity;
- continue to be good role models;
- expose students daily to a variety of good literature;
- provide listening centers with music, tapes, records, and read-along books;
- create opportunities for purposeful listening, for example, discussing, and planning activities and centers with students.

Grades 3/4

Active listening will involve growth in two areas. One is developing skills such as concentration, following directions, recognizing main and supporting details, and making inferences, judgements, and generalizations. The other is helping students become more appreciative listeners. Teachers:

- provide listening centers with tapes, simple books, and more complex novel sets;
- read aloud daily an increasing variety of lengthier good literature — myths, legends, novels;
- structure specific activities to develop listening skills;
- give increasingly complex instructions.

Grades 5/6

Teachers promote the skill of critical listening. They:

- structure opportunities to share information, opinions among peers;
- help students to appreciate individual points of view;
- provide opportunities for students to record what they hear;
- give increasingly complex instructions;
- help develop strategies for better listening.

Speaking

Kindergarten

Students need daily chances to develop their speaking skills. To facilitate language growth, teachers:

- provide learning centers and activities such as big blocks, sand and water tables, puppet theaters, dress-up centers, construction toys, puzzles, art centers, housekeeping and theme centers to stimulate student conversation;
- continually introduce new materials to centers to stimulate thinking and talking;
- have daily whole group talking times, for example, show and tell, calendar, Magic Circle;
- act as a good language model;
- question students about their experiences to help them clarify meaning.

Grade 1

Students use oral language to share thoughts and feelings with confidence and clarity. To promote vocabulary development and extension of language facility, teachers:

- structure daily sharing times/discussions based on individual and class experiences;
- promote student conversation through learning centers, for example: sand, water, reading, puppet, math;
- through activities such as construction toys provide drama and role playing experiences
- structure group speaking situations using chants and Big Books — nursery rhymes are a good language model;
- encourage students' questions.

Grade 2

Students need opportunities to extend their oral language. To serve as good role models and provide opportunities for conversation, teachers:

- structure role playing, drama, choral speaking, musical activities, Magic Circle, interviewing;
- build in problem-solving situations;
- provide centers, for example: sand, water, math, writing, art, science interest, and more teacher-directed activity centers;
- offer activities such as construction toys;
- draw out language from everyday experiences, field trips, reading materials.

Grades 3/4

Teachers provide opportunities for meaningful talk and vocabulary development. They:

- structure group activities to promote discussion/conversation, for example: planning time, role playing, interviewing, cooperative story telling, drama, choral speaking, group work;
- question students to help them extend their vocabulary and clarify meaning;
- promote purposeful conversation through interest centers, math tables, library corners, art centers, games, science tables;
- create theme units and centers involving specific learning;
- teach students to use audio/visual equipment to record stories, information, presentations;
- use field trips and students' experiences to promote language growth.

Grades 5/6

To develop and refine oral language, teachers provide opportunities for students to:

- present book reports, research information, problem solve, plan activities, share experiences;
- participate in class meetings;
- provide leadership models for younger students;
- structure formal and informal activities to develop concentration, recall;
- provide opportunities for role playing, choral reading, chants.

Reading

Kindergarten

Students begin to appreciate, use, and enjoy books. Teachers:

- visit the school library with their students regularly;
- read good quality, varied literature to students daily;
- encourage students to recognize their names and common objects in the room;

- provide a variety of pre-reading activities, for example, recognizing sequence, tell details;
- provide musical experiences and songs;
- encourage students' questions;
- expand on students' own experiences and interests.

Grade 1

Teachers begin guided reading instruction in Grade 1. They:

- provide a variety of relevant materials and experiences, for example: charts, predictable books, lists, magazines, signs, songs, basal readers, individual dictionaries, word lists;
- focus on left to right progression, the size and shape of words, letter sounds, rhyming words, word recognition in individual and small and large group situations;
- encourage students to read orally often;
- provide a classroom reading corner;
- encourage parent involvement through home reading activities.

Grade 2

Students entering Grade 2 may be at different levels and may need further reinforcement work at their level. Teachers, to develop reading skills:

- provide a variety of print materials, for example: charts, lists, recipes, newspapers, graphs, student-made and commercial books;
- direct silent and oral reading lessons, for example: basal readers, repetitive books, easy-to-read books;
- use a variety of techniques to help students develop word recognition and comprehension skills;
- integrate reading skills throughout all areas of the curriculum;
- continue home reading programs with parents.

Grades 3/4

Students at this level read for enjoyment and to gain information. Teachers build on the abilities students bring from the earlier grades. They:

- provide a variety of reading materials, for example: magazines, charts, diagrams, maps, novel sets, basal readers, newspapers, catalogues, chants, songs;
- give formal reading instruction to individuals and in large and small groups to teach specific skills, for example: comparison, evaluation, analysis, inference, judgement, prediction, values;
- begin research activities using a number of resources and methods of presentation;
- emphasize the necessity of using reading as a tool in other curriculum areas;
- encourage wider recreational reading habits.

Grades 5/6

Reading skills are integrated into all subject areas. Teachers:

- provide relevant oral reading opportunities regularly, for example, student reporting of research, presenting of projects;
- create opportunities for students to read for different purposes, for example: reading for enjoyment, comprehension, information;
- offer structured skill building activities, basal readers, novel sets to develop the mechanics where necessary;
- encourage students to develop outside reading habits.

Writing

Kindergarten

Students start to see the need for writing. Teachers:

- provide a variety of writing materials in the learning centers, such as different-shaped paper, stamp pads, little booklets, felt pens, crayons, dictionaries;
- give students experiences forming letters and words using a variety of materials, such as Plasticene, paint, crayons;
- allow students to begin the writing process through scribbling, under-writing, overcopying, or dictated stories;
- publish individual and group stories.

Grade 1

The program emphasizes the mechanical skill of printing and the recording of students' ideas and thoughts. Students' own language experiences are generated through dictated stories and independent writing. Teachers:

- provide daily directed printing instruction, moving from large, tactile printing activities like Plasticene and sandpaper to pencil and lined paper work;
- structure daily writing activities in a variety of forms and for different purposes, for example: journals, dictionaries, theme books;
- use a variety of techniques and materials such as dictionaries and word charts to help students become aware of standard spelling, spacing, left to right progression.

Grade 2

The writing program emphasizes developing independent creative writing, legibility skills, and language structure awareness. Teachers:

- continue to provide daily writing opportunities in a variety of forms;
- help students recognize the different purposes for writing, for example, to record information, retell an event;
- have cooperative writing experiences to expand stories;
- provide daily formal printing activities;
- use students' language to explore phonetic skills, spelling, parts of speech, punctuation;
- introduce editing through teacher/student conferences, group discussion, and independent proofreading.

Grades 3/4

Students write to record personal experiences, feelings, and information to develop greater clarity and sensitivity. They do different types of writing — the purpose determines the form. To promote writing, teachers:

- provide models of good writing;
- continue to provide a variety of daily writing activities;

- encourage originality and style in creative writing by following the steps of the writing process, writing models, conferences;
- teach structure (grammar, spelling, punctuation) through students' own writing and specific exercises;
- help students' writing develop and expand from words to phrases to sentences and finally to paragraphs;
- focus on skills, for example: syllabication, suffixes, prefixes, blend vowels, dictionary skills;
- introduce cursive writing in Grade 3;
- reinforce and provide practice in letter formation in Grade 4.

Grades 5/6

Writing is an effective means of communicating feelings, ideas and information. In order to develop clarity of expression, teachers:

- continue to provide regular and varied writing opportunities;
- promote spelling skills through students' writing, texts, dictionary work;
- teach the structure of language (grammar) through individual conferencing, small group or whole class lessons;
- stimulate writing through films, books, discussions, performances;
- assist students in revising, editing, and publishing their work;
- have formal or incidental lessons reinforcing cursive writing and penmanship skills.

Bibliography

Brighton, Catherine. *Five Secrets in a Box*. Markham, Ontario: Fitzhenry and Whiteside Limited, 1987.

Brownlie, Faye, Susan Close and Linda Wingren. *Tomorrow's Classroom Today*. Markham, Ontario: Pembroke Publishers/Portsmouth, New Hampshire: Heinemann Educational Books Inc., 1990.

Doake, David. "An Overview of Suggestions to be Made for Those Parents Who Want To Help Their Children Learn to Read." *Reading Manitoba*, Vol. 3, pp. 11–14, Spring 1981.

Doake, David. "Roles in Literacy Learning: A New Perspective." *International Reading Association Journal*, 1986.

Epstein, Joyce. "Parent Reactions to Teacher Practices of Parent Involvement." *Elementary School Journal*, Vol. 86, #3, January 1986.

Forester, Anne D., Margaret Reinhard. *The Learner's Way*. Winnipeg, Manitoba: Peguis Publishers, 1989.

Gasson, John, Paul Baxter. *Getting the Most Out of Your Child's School*. Toronto, Ontario: McGraw Hill Ryerson, 1989.

Golenbock, Peter. *Teammates*. San Diego, California: Harcourt Brace Jovanovich, 1990.

Hart-Hewins, Linda, Jan Wells. *Borrow A Book*. Richmond Hill, Ontario: Scholastic Books, 1988.

Hiller M., M. Lundquist. "Getting Parental Support for Your School." *Principal*, Vol. 69, #3, pp. 41–42, January 1990.

Henderson, A., C. Marlburger, T. Ooms. *Beyond the Bake Sale*. Columbia, Maryland: National Committee for Citizens in Education, 1986.

Jouard, Sidney. *Disclosing Man to Himself*. Princeton, New Jersey: Van Nostrand Reinhold, 1986.

Kennedy, Carole. "Parent Involvement: It Takes Pep." *Principal*, Vol. 70, #4, pp. 25, 27–28, March 1991.

Kerr Stenmark, Jean, Virginia Thompson, Ruth Cossey. *Family Math*. Berkeley, California: Regents, University of California, 1986.

Moffett, James, Betty Jane Wagner. *Student Centred Language Arts and Reading, K-13*. Boston, Massachusetts: Houghton Mifflin Company, 1983.

Nicole, Vivienne, Lyn Wilkie. *Literacy at Home and School*. Australia: Primary English Teachers' Association, 1990.

Purkey, William, John Novaks. *Inviting School Success*. Belmont, California: Wadsworth, 1984.

Rich, Dorothy. *Mega Skills*. Boston, Massachusetts: Houghton Mifflin Company, 1988.

Rhodes, Lynn, Curt Dudley-Marley. *Readers and Writers with a Difference*. Portsmouth, New Hampshire: Heinneman Educational Books Inc., 1988.

Ziegler, Suzanne. "The Effects of Parent Involvement on Children's Achievement: The Significance of Home/School Links." Toronto Board of Education document, 1987.

Index